AN ILLUSTRATED HISTORY OF

NEW MEXICO

AN ILLUSTRATED HISTORY OF
NEW MEXICO

Thomas E. Chávez

University of New Mexico Press
Albuquerque

© 1992 by the University Press of Colorado
First University of New Mexico Press paperback edition 2002
Published by arrangement with the University Press of Colorado

Library of Congress Cataloging-in-Publication Data

Chavez, Thomas E.
An illustrated history of New Mexico / Thomas E. Chavez.—
1st University of New Mexico Press pbk. ed.
p. cm.
Includes bibliographical references and index.
ISBN 0-8263-3051-7 (pbk. : alk. paper)
1. New Mexico—History—Pictorial works. 2. New Mexico—History. I. Title.
F797 .C47 2002
978.9—dc21
2002067306

This book is dedicated to Mark E. Chávez,
a "brother" in every sense of the word

Contents

Preface

A few years ago, an editor from a publishing company other than the original publisher of this book approached me about doing a photographic history of New Mexico. As with any mention of photographs together with history, I immediately referred that editor to Dr. Richard Rudisill of the Palace of the Governors in Santa Fe. My idea was to have Dr. Rudisill co-author the book with me, which obviously was a fit of audacity on my part. However, Dr. Rudisill was enthused with the idea of the book and agreed to help, though not in the official capacity of co-author.

With Dr. Rudisill's suggestions for photographs, his idea to use contemporary quotes interspersed with the photographs, his invaluable editorial help, and, above all, his constant encouragement, a book formulated. I, as the sole author, benefited more than words can express from my unacknowledged co-author. For, in the end, we created an illustrated history far different from that envisioned by my original inquiring editor. We created a book of melodic lines, each interesting in its own train of thought, that together create a harmony of the whole, permitting the reader/listener's mind to make its own connections.

An Illustrated History of New Mexico is intended to stimulate the reader into the realms of discovery. The beginning narrative provides a basic overview of New Mexico's past. The rest of the book is compiled from contemporary sources: photographs and quotes. The reader is encouraged to use both sources, for each will tell a tale on its own, while together they will supplement and, in some cases, amplify each other. In a sense, this book is not intended to feed the reader with information so much as to stimulate questions, connections, and ideas from the words and images of yesteryear's New Mexico.

In other words, the quotes, if read alone, will tell a tale that, like a melodic line, will complement another melodic line created by the photographic images. At times these lines may touch or cross, but they will always harmonize, for the score is about New Mexico. How the music is heard and what harmonic nuances are derived is left strictly to the listener/reader. It is my hope that this book will provoke the discovery of divergent propinquities in New Mexico's history and thus be uniquely appreciated, like good music, by each reader.

In a compilation of historical photographs there is inevitably some variation in style and condition among the pictures. Time erodes images even as it does the realities they reflect; here, we are more often left with hints and recollections than total experiences. Despite these limitations, photographs still provide us with more thorough and characteristic impressions of the past than do most other forms of recording, even with the marks of time. For this reason it has seemed best to accept the pictures of this book in the condition in which they have come to us from their time to ours.

Since most of these pictures have come from public collections, readers may wish to have information by which to acquire copies of some of them. Negative numbers have been included for most, and the following abbreviations have been used to designate sources not otherwise mentioned in detail:

POG/MNM: Palace of the Governors, Museum of New Mexico (Photo Archives, P.O. Box 2087, Santa Fe, New Mexico, 87504)

BRM/MNM: Black Range Museum Collections in the Museum of New Mexico

HSNM/MNM: Historical Society of New Mexico Collections in the Museum of New Mexico

SAR/MNM: School of American Research Collections in the Museum of New Mexico

SFRC/MNM: Santa Fe Railway Company Collections in the Museum of New Mexico

SVH/MNM: St. Vincent's Hospital Collection in the Museum of New Mexico

RGHC: Rio Grande Historical Collection (Special Collections, New Mexico State University Library, Box 3475, Las Cruces, New Mexico, 88003)

MOIFA: Museum of International Folk Art, Museum of New Mexico

Like the photographs, the quotes have been compiled mostly from sources contemporary with the historical events. All of the quotes have come from public collections or published books.

Thanks are due to a number of people without whom this volume would not have been possible. Dr. Richard Rudisill has been my colleague at the Palace of the Governors for many years. He is one of a valued staff, most of whom have worked with me for several years. Their presence at the workplace creates a tranquil environment that this museum administrator and historian has found conducive to accepting the challenge of doing books such as this. For that opportunity, I am profoundly grateful.

Then there is the subtle encouragement of loved ones. My daughters, Nicolasa Marie and Christel Angelica, enjoy the adventure of discovery that this book intends to create. They have been a part of all my publications and have even partaken in the joy of research simply by asking, "What did you find today, Daddy?" Being prepared to answer that question is a task gladly fulfilled.

No one has worked for me and with me longer or harder than my parents, Judge Antonio E. Chávez and Marilyn Sprowl Chávez. Anything I accomplish is theirs. They, along with Richard Rudisill, are silent co-authors. Also, the solid computer and editorial work of Karen Gordon, who is also a staff member, is of special benefit.

The publisher of the first editions of this book, the University Press of Colorado, was selected because I had learned through the experience of a previous publication with the Press that a book attempting to do something different would be secure in the hands of its capable and professional staff.

Now the University of New Mexico has taken on the task of publishing this edition and, on the face of it, nothing could be more natural—a history of New Mexico published by the premier press in New Mexico. But there is more than meets the eye, for while others have helped with the making of this book, one has not been mentioned. Besides myself, only my friend and, I am proud to say, colleague Luther Wilson has been with this book since its inception. Actually, the idea for an illustrated history was originally his and it was he who sent the inquiries mentioned in the beginning of this preface, so Luther's relationship with this publication predates me. And, he was the only individual who encouraged, supported, and indeed, published all the editions. Not surprisingly, then, one of his first moves after becoming director of the University of New Mexico Press was to begin the process of reissuing *An Illustrated History of New Mexico*. The book is as much his as mine. He is indeed an advocate of New Mexico's patrimony.

Years after the first edition was published, this book will continue to teach. Photographs and the words of yesteryear are timeless. With the passage of time those mementos become invaluable and when brought together offer a window on the past much larger than the total that their individual value would indicate. The popularity of the earlier editions is a testimony to the value of such a conduit to the past. The University of New Mexico Press has assured that more people will have the opportunity to view, and learn from, our predecessors, our ancestors. So this book is a lesson, in great part self-teaching as you read and look through it. Like a seed, I hope that this book will join others to grow in a garden that will bloom with understanding and appreciation for a better future.

An Illustrated History of New Mexico is a compilation of photographs, illustrations, and quotations. It is the end result of a selection process, which means that not everything is included in the final product. There are more omissions than inclusions. Every person who reads or views this book will undoubtedly know of a photograph or quotation that was omitted. I accept responsibility for such seemingly bad taste. But those who question the result of the selection have been snookered, for in getting to the point of questioning the book's contents, the reader has been required to think about what has been read. And that, after all, is the intent of this volume.

Thomas E. Chávez

An Illustrated History of New Mexico

Prologue: A Historical Synopsis

Most people in the United States learn their country's history with virtually no mention of Hispanic influence save that of Christopher Columbus, who probably was a Genoese-Italian sailing under the Spanish colors. They learn a story of early exploration and settlement by a few English religious separatists and commercial adventurers who encountered woodlands Indians on the East Coast. From the seed of these initial, small, and successful settlements grew a powerful transcontinental nation, the story goes. Traditional U.S. history is a tale of European civilization expanding and developing as it progressed through a frontier filter from the East Coast to the West Coast. But alongside these events, a narrative of another European people in the New World unfolded. Spain actually had claimed and begun settlement of the New World some sixty years prior to official English attempts at settlement. Like their neighbors, the Spaniards confronted a wilderness and new people. They, too, settled and expanded. The seeds of Spanish civilization reached into Central and South America and north into the present-day southwestern and southeastern United States. The story of Hispanic colonization in North America contains many similarities to that of English colonization. Spanish culture, likewise, became distinctly American as it grew from its European roots through a New World wilderness experience.

Within four centuries after Columbus sailed, the predominantly English civilization of the East Coast met the Spanish civilization of the southwest. The focal point of this significant meeting was northern New Mexico. Geographical circumstances determined that the area would be the hub of this cultural encounter.

For a majority of its existence, New Mexico truly was an island in the wilderness settled beyond the respective frontiers of both the Spanish-Mexican empire and the United States. Until the middle of the nineteenth century, settlements in the region were virtually cut off from civilization. Between northern New Mexico and the silver mining outposts of the Mexican frontier lay approximately one thousand miles of hostile territory occupied by nomadic Indians. New Mexico was equally distant from the approaching American frontier, which had reached the Mississippi Valley.

New Mexicans were never completely isolated, however. They did correspond and trade with their distant relatives, although supply caravans sometimes did not arrive for as long as three years because of distance and hardship. Church and military supplies took precedence over private considerations, so utilitarian goods for settlers were rare. Over the years, New Mexicans learned to do things on their own, and in the process they developed independent attitudes along with a culture somewhat different from the strong neo-Aztec strains of Mexico proper. They had to learn to survive in a harsh land against high odds with very little help from the seats of European civilizations.

The Hispanic settlers of New Mexico did receive help from the indigenous Indian population. Governor Don Juan de Oñate's first colonists took up lodging in Indian pueblos, and Indian goods such as blankets and bowls quickly permeated the households of the new settlers. The Indians, especially the Pueblos, had much knowledge to share about surviving in New Mexico's unforgiving environment. When the Spaniards arrived, Pueblo society was growing enough foodstuff to store an overage. In addition to farming, the Pueblos traded with the many nomadic Indian groups that lived around them. The villages located on the frontier of Pueblo land participated in such trade a little more extensively. Evidence of Pueblo goods as far away as the Mississippi River valley and central Mexico as well as items imported from Mexico and the West Coast give testimony to the far-reaching trade of the native New Mexicans.

After Mexican Independence in 1821, New Mexico became a cosmopolitan frontier outpost. American civilization had expanded to the Mississippi Valley, sending its forerunners fur trapping into the Rocky Mountains. St. Louis merchants quickly realized that Santa Fe and Taos, New Mexico, both in the southern Rockies, were in geographical locations that could be beneficial to trade. Employees of fur companies could deposit their wares in New Mexico for shipment over the newly opened Santa Fe Trail east to Missouri. Other things besides trade goods crossed the plains between Mexico and the

United States. The international caravans also conveyed people and their mores. Because New Mexico served as a frontier outpost for both cultures, it became a place where Americans, Spaniards now become Mexicans, Indians, and even remnants of the early French made up a multifaceted society.

Historians have traditionally divided New Mexico's history into six major periods: prehistory, Spanish exploration, the colonial period, the Mexican years, the territorial years, and statehood. The first period, prehistory, refers to the time before European contact, during which Indian civilization flourished throughout the Southwest. New Mexico's prehistory dates from 12,000 B.C. or earlier.

Modern scholars do not have the benefit of the written word in reconstructing the area's early cultures. Instead they must rely upon the study of material remains. New Mexico, fortunately, has been an archaeological gold mine for such detective work. Discoveries such as the Folsom Site in eastern New Mexico, the Sandia Cave near Albuquerque, and the Clovis Site near the Anderson Basin have given testimony to early occupation in New Mexico.

Four thousand years later, during the last phase of the Ice Age, the people of the Southwest started hunting less and gathering wild foods more. By 3000 B.C., cultural differences developed between the southern nomadic people and the more sedentary folk in the Four Corners area. And ideas, especially agricultural ones from Mexican cultures, were being adopted in New Mexico, initiating a long-lasting trend. As the people became more attached to their farms, time became available to make pottery, develop architectural styles, and evolve decorations for ceramics, or walls. The people of southern New Mexico have been labeled the Mogollon culture, while the northerners have become known as the Anasazi.

The Mogollon, probably because of their closer proximity to Mexico, developed before the Anasazi. Village life was introduced to the Four Corners region around A.D. 250, after which the Anasazi began to evolve. By A.D. 1000 they had surpassed the Mogollon, with larger communities and more advanced architectural techniques. The Anasazi economy included surface mining for hematite, turquoise, and obsidian, as well as trade with societies as far away as the Pacific Coast and central Mexico. Remnants of their magnificent villages can be seen in Chaco Canyon — where Pueblo Bonito, the largest such ruin in North America, stands in mute testimony to a glorious period — and at other sites, such as the Salmon and Aztec ruins. These, like the hundreds of village sites in Chaco Canyon, were multistoried villages built around an enclosed plaza with a circular ceremonial chamber. The large populations were sustained by crops and water derived from complex irrigation systems. Their ideas spread west into the Rio Grande valley, which developed more slowly.

Coupled with ideas and migrants from the Mogollon society, the Rio Grande civilizations began to develop. A drought in the thirteenth century forced many, if not most, of the Anasazi people to move west to the Rio Grande, where the pueblo villages began to develop into larger communities in places like Bandelier, Puyé, Castle (on the Chama River), and other locales. By 1300 pueblos were built in many outlying areas east of the river, including Pecos, Gran Quivira, and Quarai. In all of these areas, the Anasazi established important trade relations with the Plains Indians.

Most of the pueblos that survived into historic times date to the drought of the late 1200s. While some were abandoned during another drought in the late 1500s — for example, the pueblos of Bandelier National Monument — most of the pueblos extant today date from this period.

When the Spanish arrived in the first half of the sixteenth century, they encountered Indian villages of multistoried dwellings built on a square or rectangular ground plan around the central plaza. Taos, consisting of two house blocks separated by a plaza, is a notable exception. The Spanish also found domesticated dogs, turkeys, and extensive farmlands. More important, they met a sedentary people they considered ripe for conversion to Christianity.

Spanish exploration and discovery began the second phase of New Mexico's history. This phase was launched in 1521 when Hernán Cortés laid siege to the Aztec capital of Tenochtitlán (Mexico City) and initiated the subsequent search for "other Mexicos." In the tradition of the recently completed reconquest of the Iberian Peninsula, these Spanish adventurers set off on a quest to find new civilizations, wealth, and cities beyond their wildest imaginations. Cortés's soldiers were amazed at what they discovered. One of the soldiers, Bernal Diaz del Castillo, perhaps best captured the awe of his countrymen when he wrote:

> We arrived at a broad Causeway and continued our march . . . and when we
> saw so many cities and villages built in the water and other great towns on
> dry land and that straight and level Causeway going towards Mexico [City],

we were amazed and said that it was like the enchantment they tell of in the legend of Amadis, on account of the great towers and cues [temples] and buildings rising from the water, and all built of masonry. And some of our soldiers even asked whether the things that we saw were not a dream. . . . [T]here is so much to think over that I do not know how to describe it, seeing things as we did that had never been heard of or seen before, not even dreamed about.

Soon after the discovery and conquest of Tenochtitlán, Spanish explorers found and conquered the great Inca civilization of Perú in South America. Attention then turned toward the lands north of New Mexico, for it was the only direction still uncharted. Many Spaniards felt that another wealthy, established civilization must lie to the north, and they sent expeditions to find it.

The search for wealth was coupled with Papal dispensation for Spain to convert all newly discovered pagans to the Holy Mother Catholic Church. In the Treaty of Tordesillas of 1496, the Pope audaciously divided the world between Portugal and Spain. The only real condition imposed was that the natives be converted. Spain had found new souls along with riches in the south and now looked for more. The desire for northern exploration increased with rumors of people living in established cities.

Obviously, stable populations tended to accumulate more wealth than nomadic peoples. More pertinent to New Mexico's story, however, is that Spanish missionaries found sedentary people more convenient for conversion. When people lived in towns, a church could be easily placed among the inhabitants. Nomadic Indians, on the other hand, would have to be kept virtual prisoners, for they had no permanent homes. Priests would have to gather nomadic Indians and forcibly keep them around the church to learn an alien lifestyle. The clergy found conversion and education much easier with Indians who lived in a village next to the church.

The 1536 expedition to Florida led by Pánfilo de Narváez resulted in an official push to explore the north. Four survivors of that expedition had shipwrecked on the Texas coast and wandered across south central Texas and northern Mexico before being rescued by Spanish slave hunters. These survivors, led by Alvar Núñez Cabeza de Vaca and including the Moorish slave Estevanico, heard tales of people to the north who lived in cities and houses of more than two stories high. Such stories had an added luster, for they seemed to confirm Aztec mythology, which told of that great people's ancestors coming from a land to the north, a land called Aztlán. The viceroy of New Spain commissioned two subsequent expeditions that both confirmed and dispelled expectations. There were indeed cities, but they contained no wealth. In fact, the first expedition, led by Fray Marcos de Niza, resulted in the death of the Moor Estevanico and even greater tales of wealth. The subsequent 1540–1542 expedition of Francisco Vásquez de Coronado went all the way to present-day Lyons, Kansas, on the Arkansas River in pursuit of the illusive Quivira, the cities of gold. While failing to find Quivira, Coronado's army gained a tremendous amount of geographical, botanical, and demographical knowledge.

Silver discoveries and the resulting Chichimec Indian Wars in the Zacatecas area of north central Mexico caused a forty-year delay before the next round of expeditions. These explorations were undertaken by members of the Franciscan order. The first, led by Fray Agustín Rodríquez with Captain Francisco Sánchez Chamuscado in 1581, resulted in the martyrdom of Rodríquez and his fellow priests, who had remained in New Mexico. The next year, Antonio de Espejo and Fray Bernaldino Baltrán led a second expedition and returned after determining the fate of the priests from the Rodríquez foray. In 1590, in an illegal attempt to establish a Spanish settlement, Gaspar Castaño de Sosa entered New Mexico without permission from the viceroy. Castaño was quickly followed by Juan Morlete, who arrested him. Castaño was taken back in chains and sentenced to serve on Manila Galleon, on which he died. A couple of years later, Captain Francisco Leyva de Bonilla and his partner, Juan de Humaña, led a second illegal expedition into New Mexico. Both men were killed, Bonilla by his own men and Humaña by Indians.

Historians have called these expeditions the "rediscovery of New Mexico" because they resulted from a renewed interest and activity that ended with the settlement of the area. The first successful settlement occurred in 1598 at San Juan de los Caballeros under the leadership of Governor Don Juan de Oñate. The people were sent for the primary purpose of converting Indian souls; nonetheless, other motives existed, not the least of which was the possibility of finding the Straits of Anian (the Northwest Passage) somewhere north of New Mexico. Harsh winters, Oñate's lack of attention to his colony's basic needs, and his own cruel disciplinary tactics led to complaints from the colonists. He eventually fell into official disfavor and in 1609 was succeeded as governor by Pedro de Peralta, who had instructions to move to a more central location and establish a village that would be called Santa Fe.

Oñate's 1598 settlement began the Spanish Colonial period, which continued until Mexican Independence in 1821. For almost two and a quarter centuries, New Mexico existed as an outpost of the Spanish Empire. Life was hard. Settlers had to survive with little help from the governments of Mexico (New Spain) or Spain. They also had to protect themselves from Indian raids. The church and civil authorities were required to share power, and that caused governmental problems. Governors would not aid priests in their missionizing efforts, and priests became very adept at making life miserable for the civil officials. Both factions competed for the loyalty of settlers and Indians who were, in turn, caught in the middle of the church-state feud. To be sure, there were abuses of power on both sides. Governors and priests were recalled to Mexico, where some had to defend themselves before the Inquisition.

In 1625 Alonso de Benavides arrived in New Mexico as the new father custodian, with the authority of the offices of the Inquisition and, more important, a small statue of Mary. The statue was originally called "Our Lady of the Assumption" but later became "Our Lady of the Rosary" (Nuestra Señora del Rosario). She quickly became popular with a *cofradia* formed in her honor. She also acquired the affectionate name of "Nuestra Señora de la Conquistadora." Her name did not honor a conquest because there had been none, but the people used the word in a formal sense of "conquering" or winning one's affections, and unifying.

Father Benavides remained in New Mexico less than five years; however, when he left he became one of the area's earliest boosters. He wrote a memoir that he presented to King Felipe IV in 1630 and revised to present to Pope Urban VIII in 1635. A most interesting tidbit in Benavides's long report is the story of María de Agreda, a Spanish nun and mystic, who miraculously appeared before nomadic Indian tribes and thus confirmed New Mexico as a chosen place in the eyes of God. The bi-locating "Lady in Blue" has become a southwestern legend.

New Mexico had its share of villains, too. Probably the most notorious was Governor Diego de Peñalosa, who had been convicted of murder in Perú before his appointment. As governor he fabricated an expedition for which he listed himself the leader. For his constant verbal abuse and resistance to the clergy as well as his high-handed manner, he was arrested, charged with insubordination and blasphemy, and deported from the Spanish empire.

In spite of Peñalosa's crimes, society prospered. Exploration and conversion continued. Some voyagers traveled as far as the Gulf of California and into Kansas. New cities were founded. As society developed and families grew, people came to call New Mexico home.

Perhaps the most significant event of the Colonial period was the Pueblo Indian Revolt of 1680. In the most successful native rebellion against Europeans in North American history, the Pueblo Indians, with some aid from neighboring nomadic tribes, forced the Spanish into exile for thirteen years. (The area the Indians overtook stretched from north-central Arizona to south-central New Mexico.) Spanish survivors took refuge in El Paso del Norte district, where they continued to communicate with factions of the victorious Indians and even made a few attempts to retake their "homeland." Not until Don Diego de Vargas became governor did the exiles have success. In 1692 Vargas, who dedicated the resettlement to the little statue of Mary he affectionately called "la Conquista," led an army into New Mexico and, without a violent conflict, met with various Pueblo emissaries, usually over cups of hot chocolate, to prepare the way for the subsequent return of the colonists. His peaceful *entrada,* or entry, was astounding enough to result in a book written by famous historian Carlos de Sigüenza y Góngora. Unfortunately, the second campaign a year later met with Indian resistance at Santa Fe. With the help of Pecos Pueblo auxiliaries, Vargas forcibly occupied Santa Fe. The capital had to be rebuilt. San Miguel Church had to be reroofed because the old one had collapsed in the fires of the Pueblo Revolt. The old parish church had been completely demolished, so a new one was built, and la Conquistadora was placed in her "temple," where she remains today.

The Spanish came back wiser for their errors. Both they and their Pueblo adversaries realized that they had a common enemy: the nomadic Indians who raided farming communities, especially at harvest time. As populations expanded throughout the Rio Grande drainage, raids from Apache, Ute, Comanche, and Navajo Indians became increasingly burdensome. Spanish settlers with Pueblo Indian auxiliaries fought back, but not until the 1780s, under the leadership of Governor Juan Bautista de Anza, could any success be claimed. Anza rode out to the eastern plains of southern Colorado and defeated the great Comanche leader, Cuerno Verde, in his own territory. He then used Comanche aid to defeat the Apaches in eastern New Mexico.

The conquest of nomadic tribes enabled colonial society to expand. The *Rio Abajo* settlements spread down the Rio Grande with astonishing rapidity in a period of growth and social stabilization. The pastoral and farming society was pretty much self-sustaining. Flocks of sheep went to the mining districts of north central Mexico. Buffalo hides were also packed south. Throughout the eighteenth century, the *Rio Abajo* began to give rise to wealthy individuals by New Mexican standards. With the proliferation of towns, new churches were built. Local artists painted saints and scenes on wood or hide. Statues, also of wood, were made to adorn churches, chapels, and homes. For the first time, the Bishop of Durango was interested enough to make a tour of inspection to New Mexico.

Under King Carlos III and his Inspector General, José de Gálvez, the whole Spanish northern frontier was reorganized into the *Provincias Internas* (Internal Provinces) as part of the Bourbon Reforms in the late eighteenth century. This reorganization condensed New Spain's northern territories to approximately the current international border, which left New Mexico projecting beyond the established frontier line and, as usual, with little aid or encouragement from the central government.

At the same time, French traders started violating Spain's mercantilist policy of closed borders. As early as the 1730s, Frenchmen wandered into New Mexican settlements from the upper Mississippi and Ohio River valleys. Some even came from Canada to seek trade with New Mexico, albeit illegally. A few survivors from the ill-fated expedition of René-Robert Cavelier sieur de La Salle were stranded on the Texas coast and ended up in New Mexico to leave their names and progeny. With reports of Frenchmen from the Illinois country trading on the fringes of the Spanish empire, the punitive campaigns against nomadic Indians evolved into a search for French intruders. The most famous of these journeys was sent out by Governor Antonio de Valverde in 1720. Under the command of Pedro de Villasur, the expedition traveled to the confluence of the Platte and Loup rivers, where he and a majority of his men died in an ambush of French and Pawnee and Oto Indians.

The conclusion of the French and Indian War in 1763 ended France's influence in North America and left the continent divided between Great Britain and Spain at the Mississippi River. Many Frenchmen in America had grown used to the frontier and preferred to become Spanish citizens rather than return to Europe. French explorers and Indian traders now worked under Spanish auspices. Not the least of these Frenchmen-turned-Spanish citizens was Don Pedro Vial, a pedestrian who had traversed the land between New Orleans and Santa Fe. He then walked from Santa Fe to Missouri in eighteen days in a trek hinting at the eventual Santa Fe Trail.

After the turn of the nineteenth century, New Mexico sent a representative to the Spanish *cortes,* or parliament, to petition for aid. The success of his trip gave birth to one of the most often quoted jingles in New Mexico's history: *"Don Pedro Pino fué, Don Pedro Pino vino,"* (Don Pedro Pino went, Don Pedro Pino returned). Pedro Bautista Pino's reports and requests came to no avail; Spain had passed its days of glory and power and could do nothing more than listen to his pleas. Indeed, within a few more years, Spain would lose all her colonies in the Americas, including the province of New Mexico.

For New Mexico, the most significant aspect of Mexican Independence in 1821 was the major change in policy toward foreign commerce. Under Spanish rule, trade with other nations was forbidden. American traders and soldiers such as Zebulon M. Pike (who entered New Mexico in 1807) were arrested and returned to the United States. Under the new Republic of Mexico, the borders were opened for trade. New Mexico's close proximity to the United States' western frontier made it an important port of entry for American fur trappers and traders. The Santa Fe Trail, a route traversing the prairies from Missouri to northern New Mexico, irretrievably turned New Mexico's attention to the United States. Where once supply caravans from Mexico arrived at intervals as great as three years, now numerous caravans came to Santa Fe every year. Each arrival created a bustle of excitement, for it brought useful goods long considered rare. Even so, this was not exclusively an American enterprise. About half the trade over the Santa Fe Trail was run by Mexican citizens at the time the Mexican War broke out in 1846. Many of these Mexicans had also received some of their education in St. Louis.

One man deeply involved in international commerce, a Rio Abajo *rico* named Manuel Armijo, served as governor on three different occasions during this period. He successfully led the loyal forces that ended the short-lived 1837 revolt staged by José Gonzales of Taos. He was also the governor when the infamous 1841 Texas expedition was captured and marched to prison in Mexico. (Texas sought to open trade with New Mexico and solidify its western border claims by sending more than three hundred men and fourteen wagons to Santa Fe. Mexico found Texas's claims to the Rio Grande outlandish because, among other things, this would have included all of New Mexico east of the river. The ill-planned, misdirected expedition never succeeded as it straggled into New Mexico's outer settlements, where it was "captured.") Armijo was governor, once again, when the United States Army of the West, commanded by Brig. Gen. Stephen Watts Kearny, arrived during the Mexican War. On this occasion Armijo was not victorious. For reasons still debated, the governor offered no resistance to the American army. He fled south instead, leaving New Mexico open to a successful American invasion.

New Mexico's Mexican period ended when Kearny's army occupied the area. Although underground resisters violently opposed the foreign army and their sympathizers (Kearny's appointed governor, Charles Bent, was assassinated in Taos in 1847), Mexico ceded New Mexico to the United States with the Treaty of Guadalupe Hidalgo in 1848. In the famous congressional compromise of 1850, the old Spanish province and Mexican department became a United States territory.

Territorial status, rather than statehood, was the result of two major problems. First, sectionalism was moving the United States to civil war, and New Mexico was caught up in the slave-state/free-state issue. Second, although New Mexico had sufficient population to qualify for statehood, the fact that the population was neither Protestant nor English-speaking caused opposition for the next sixty-two years.

The territorial years witnessed some of the biggest events in the history of both New Mexico and the United States: the Civil War, the flourishing and end of the Santa Fe Trail, a profitable sheep trade to California, the infamous political cadre known as the Santa Fe Ring, the arrival of the railroad, range wars, the Spanish-American War and the Rough Riders, a different form of Catholicism, and an end to hostile Indian activities. All this made up a complicated period during which American society passed from the tradition of the horse and buggy and gas lighting to the automotive and electric era. This transition was especially significant within New Mexico's continued frontier setting. The state's culture had different roots than the culture of the eastern seaboard. One obvious distinction was religion and its influence on society. Unlike the eastern states, New Mexico did not have the tradition or social psyche forged by the Puritan work ethic until the last half of the nineteenth century.

In many ways, Padre Antonio José Martínez of Taos personified the period in that he was torn between his own country and the growing influence of the United States. While he saw advantages and disadvantages to both countries, Martínez proved to be a Mexican patriot and part-time Armijo critic whose greatest credit was his dedication to education. Many of his students became priests and civic leaders.

Martínez, along with many of his clerical colleagues, had as his biggest problem a new church hierarchy. With the change of governments on a national level, New Mexico was separated from the Mexican Diocese of Durango, and a new ecclesiastical administration began with the appointment of French-born Jean Baptiste Lamy as Vicar Apostolic. After arriving in Santa Fe in 1851, Bishop Lamy initiated a church building program. Employing French and Italian contractors and carpenters, he built the Chapel of Loretto and Saint Francis Cathedral in Santa Fe. He also imported teachers such as the Sisters of Loretto and Members of the Christian Brothers to establish church schools. However, Lamy proceeded to cause problems with the local clergy. With his assistant, he tried to discourage the activities of the lay confraternities known as the Penitentes. The pair also unfairly criticized the local clergy to the point that Lamy's assistant had to defend his actions in Rome.

Like the rest of the nation, New Mexico was disrupted with the outbreak of the Civil War. New Mexico sided with the Union, primarily because Texas joined the Confederate States and then sent a force up the Rio Grande from El Paso to claim the territory. After a major battle at Fort Craig in southern New Mexico and a defeat at Glorieta, southeast of Santa Fe, the Texan army retreated, and the Union troops in New Mexico spent the rest of the war fighting Indians. Christopher "Kit" Carson, under orders from General James H. Carleton, embarked on a campaign in the winter of 1862–1863 to round up hostile Navajos and take them to Fort Sumner in eastern New Mexico. There, along with their traditional enemies, the Mescalero Apaches, they were to be forcibly taught the white man's ways in an army experiment that failed miserably. Both the Mescalero and Navajo were allowed to return to their homelands, never again posing a real threat. The distinction for hostile longevity belonged to Gerónimo and his renegade band of Chiricahua Apaches in southern New Mexico and Arizona, who were not subdued until 1886.

In the last quarter of the nineteenth century, social scientests rushed to record the customs of the Southwest's indigenous peoples. The Smithsonian Institution's Bureau of Ethnology sent its first field expedition to Zuni Pueblo. Among its members was Frank Hamilton Cushing, a young ethnologist whose writings about his five-year experience in Zuni became recognized as prime examples of studies in the discipline of American ethnology. John K. Hillers was the expedition's photographer, and his pictures taken throughout the Southwest are now held among the collections of the National Archives, the Smithsonian Institution, and the Museum of New Mexico.

Early archaeologist Adolph F. Bandelier made his home in Santa Fe in the 1880s and 1890s while doing field work at many prehistoric ruins in the vicinity. Charles Lummis, transcontinental pedestrian, publisher, and amateur photographer, accompanied Bandelier part of the time. While Bandelier recorded his archaeological findings and Lummis recorded impressions and images, historian Ralph Emerson Twitchell combed the archives to preserve New Mexico's history. Both Bandelier and Twitchell recognized a rich Hispanic culture and heritage, and they are considered founding fathers of their respective disciplines in the Southwest.

Even some of the federally appointed territorial governors, none of whom achieved fame for their administrative abilities, partook in intellectual pursuits. In 1880 Governor Lew Wallace completed his novel *Ben Hur*, the first biblical novel in U.S. literary history, and soon-to-be governor LeBaron Bradford Prince and some friends resurrected the Historical Society of New Mexico, which had been dormant because of the Civil War. Prince also wrote history. Edmund G. Ross, a governor who achieved more administrative success than the others, made history. He was sent to New Mexico as a form of political exile in the aftermath of his refusal to vote for Andrew Johnson's impeachment.

In 1879 the first railroad made its way into New Mexico, bringing with it the cultural baggage of the Gilded Age. The United States, flushed with pride in the wake of its 1876 centennial celebration, embarked on a period marked by chauvinistic nationalism, rapid industrial growth, a mercurial economy, and increasing urbanization. As investment and speculation became a prevalent trend, mining boomed and railroad trunk lines were routed to the various new boom towns. Some gold and silver were found; most people remained poor; some famous people (for instance, Ulysses S. Grant) visited New Mexico seeking an investment in the extractive industries. Eventually, most of the boom towns became ghost towns. Meanwhile, the railroads' intrusion into New Mexico stimulated the cattle industry. Now beef could be transported to the eastern population centers from New Mexican towns. With increased opportunities, more land was needed to raise beef. The drive for land resulted in different attitudes toward land. Rather than the more traditional community-based land uses, property became a commodity for speculation. Ownership boundaries were marked by fences that cut up open ranges. Worse, range wars erupted.

Outbreaks of violence reflected widespread lawlessness and vigilante activity. Personalities such as Pat Garrett, Billy the Kid, Clay Allison, Elfego Baca, and "Black Jack" Ketchum helped create an image of an unstable New Mexico that proponents of statehood found hard to overcome. Not even the introduction of public schools or New Mexican enlistees filling the ranks of Theodore Roosevelt's Rough Riders during the Spanish American War could bring the territory into the union. Despite promises to the contrary, New Mexico did not become a state until the end of William Howard Taft's presidential term in 1912. By then the range wars had ended, the Spanish-American War hysteria had subsided, and the "Anglo-American" population had increased, creating a ripe environment for statehood.

Statehood, the final historical period, began calmly enough. Tourism, made possible by the railroad, boomed into a major industry. Indian bowls and rugs were no longer made for utilitarian purposes but were regarded primarily as art or souvenir objects. Information gleaned from research on the Southwest led to the establishment of museums, historic sites, and an uninspiring combination of both: the curio shop. A growing urge to retain the past became most evident in the romanticism of Pueblo Revival architecture, a loose term for structures built of adobe and possibly with flat roofs. Ernest Thompson Seton, co-founder of the Boy Scouts, came to New Mexico to study and paint New Mexico's wildlife. Artists and writers fled from the eastern cities to New

Mexico's high, dry climate and unfamiliar cultures. New Mexico became a poor man's Europe, and Taos and Santa Fe developed into major art colonies.

Other elements of the past lived on. Pancho Villa's 1916 raid on Columbus, New Mexico, proved that frontier violence was still possible. His pursuit, led by General John J. Pershing, hinted at impending modern warfare with trucks and airplanes. Demographic change also took place, for the Indian and Hispanic populations were soon numerically surpassed by a rapidly growing influx of Anglo-Americans. Urbanites outnumbered rural dwellers and, perhaps indicative of such changes, cattle replaced sheep as the state's major livestock in the 1920s.

New Mexico had always been an economic drain on its mother country, be it Spain, Mexico, or the United States. American presidential administrations invariably complained that the area was a strain on the national economy, and statehood did nothing to change that situation. Ever-increasing amounts of federal money flowed into New Mexico achieving record levels during and after World War II.

Much of this money underwrote the research that heralded the nuclear age. An artificial glow brightened the morning of July 17, 1945, with the initial detonation of the atomic bomb at the Trinity Site in south central New Mexico. The secret, federally funded Manhattan Project spent $2 million to develop the bomb at Los Alamos under the direction of J. Robert Oppenheimer. This program has been followed by other similarly financed programs. The Los Alamos and Sandia Laboratories, White Sands Missile Range (where the space shuttle Columbia landed on its third voyage), and Holoman and Kirtland Air Force Bases still bolster New Mexico's economy with federal money. Not until now has New Mexico been financially beneficial to its national government. In a time of energy crisis, New Mexico's natural resources — oil, coal, gas, and uranium — have attracted a new interest.

In the twentieth century tourism grew into a major industry and had profound impact on native customs. Indian blankets, bowls, jewelry, and fetishes became items for collectors' mantel pieces or walls. The same thing happened with Santeros, creators of religious statues and paintings. New tools, new materials, and increasingly fast technological changes helped craftsmen cater to the buyer. Exaggerated colors and designs and greater production reflected the new market. The buying public helped preserve many traditional crafts, although they are no longer created for traditional reasons. Today, many New Mexican cities hold annual Spanish and Indian markets that draw thousands of people. Santa Fe's Indian market, run by the Southwest Association on Indian Affairs, attracts so many people that a good number of the locals leave town.

Many of New Mexico's "traditional" cultural traits attributed to one or the other civilization are more than likely traits in some way influenced by all. Navajo blankets are an excellent case in point. Spaniards introduced sheep and shepherding techniques to the Southwest. Indians learned to utilize wool while applying their weaving skills to create blankets with designs originally derived from both cultures. Research has found that some Navajo designs have been influenced by Saltillo *serapes* (blankets) from Mexico. These designs, in turn, exhibit an amalgamation of Spanish, Mexican, Indian, and Moorish styles. More recent blanket designs reflect the added influence of American society.

Indians sell jewelry under portals lining the old town plazas of Santa Fe and Albuquerque. They have an active market for their handcrafted silver, coral, and turquoise ornaments, yet few buyers realize that the materials, craftsmanship, and designs reflect a multifaceted heritage. Many visitors purchase jewelry in front of buildings whose architectural designs also represent a diverse heritage. The Palace of the Governors in Santa Fe, the oldest continuously used public building in the United States, received its current look during renovations in 1909–1913. The result is a building with architectural facets that reflect its many inhabitants and their tastes. Now called Pueblo or Old Santa Fe style, the design was a reaction to the growing number of Victorian edifices. This reaction resulted in a misconstrued Spanish colonial-pueblo style. In many ways, the prevalent architectural styles of New Mexico are revealing of the people, for they are a result of a long evolutionary process that embodies change, even reaction.

A narrative history of New Mexico, abridged here, cannot reveal the whole story. At times, the area's history may appear disjointed as it meanders through the centuries. That is hardly surprising, though, because to study history is to study people. It is they, beings consistent in their inconsistency, who make history.

New Mexico's history is also the story of cultural development. The

Spanish and Indian cultures have lived side by side in the American Southwest for almost four hundred years. Early Europeans borrowed from the native culture, and Indians found many advantageous qualities in the new civilization moving into their midst. But they rejected and resisted other aspects of their powerful neighbors' culture and maintained their own traditions. Relatively recently a third culture entered the area, and Hispanic and Indian societies now entered into the process of adjusting to Anglo-Americans. The influence was especially evident with the Santa Fe Trail and, eventually, the railroad, which made possible a boom that quickly changed local lifestyles.

In a very real sense, this region has been an intellectual and social recipient of the New World spirit. Expressed as Neo-Aztecism or the synthesis of Spanish and central Mexican Indian culture, this spirit is nowhere better exemplified than in the myth of Nuestra Señora de Guadalupe, for the story of her miracle helped weave the diverse elements of New Spain's vast population into one distinctive people. The appearance of the Virgin Mary to an Indian boy near Mexico City provided the majority of New Spain's native inhabitants with a rallying point sent directly from Heaven. Guadalupe then became a focus for Spain's New World subjects, for the Virgin's appearance symbolized God's personal concern for them. The story of New Mexico's Santuario de Chimayó, in northern New Mexico, reiterated the point of God's personal involvement in the colonies and for local people. The crucified Christ appeared over ground traditionally considered spiritual by the local Indian population. Today, pilgrims walk to a chapel erected on the spot, and the descendants of all the cultures have become spiritual partners.

Like the rest of the country, New Mexico has become urbanized. Albuquerque is a city with an international airport, big boulevards, and high-rise buildings. Neon advertisements, fast-food restaurants, and motels are obvious in all of New Mexico's cities. Yet New Mexico has been able to adapt new influences; its culture has always changed and will continue to do so. The great challenge today is the rapidity of change. Can a community with such a long and obvious cultural heritage, so entwined with its special climate and topography, maintain its integrity before a modern technological world? Yes, it can. The peculiarities that make New Mexico have equipped the state better to fulfill her motto to "grow as it goes." For cultural growth is a civilization's soul — and that is what makes New Mexico special.

CHAPTER 1

Those Who Were Here:
Indians and Land Before Contact

Sometimes called the prehistoric or pre-Columbian period, this is the time before Europeans arrived in New Mexico, dating from at least 12,000 B.C. until the first Spanish explorations in the sixteenth century. By the end of this period, many Indian villages had been established. The Indians farmed and even raised an abundance. Trade networks with neighboring nomadic Indians stretched from the Mississippi River valley to the Pacific Coast to the civilizations of north-central Mexico.

❖ ❖ ❖

River scene, New Mexico. Photo by T. Harmon Parkhurst. *(MNM 66679)*

❖ ❖ ❖

New Mexico sunset, ca. 1912. Photo by Jesse L. Nusbaum. *(MNM 61567)*

❖ ❖ ❖

The Rio Grande from Sandía Crest, ca. 1940. Photo by T. Harmon Parkhurst. *(MNM 66475)*

❖ ❖ ❖

Petroglyph rocks at Cienega, New Mexico. Photo ca. 1925–1930. *(MNM 42428)*
Petroglyphs. Photo ca. 1900. *(MNM 97)*

❖ ❖ ❖

Prehistoric stone figure excavated at Pecos Pueblo.
Photo by Ernest Johanson. *(MNM 44343)*

❖ ❖ ❖

Cave dwellings, Pajarito Plateau. Photo ca. 1910. *(MNM 41997)*
Tyuonyi ruins, Frijoles Canyon, 1910. Photo by Jesse L. Nusbaum. *(MNM 28693)*

❖ ❖ ❖

Petroglyphs, San Cristóbal Pueblo, 1927. Photo by Kenneth Chapman. *(MNM 38331)*

26

❖ ❖ ❖

Sandía Mountains from Kuaua Pueblo, ca. 1940. *(MNM 139724)*

❖ ❖ ❖

Katzimo (Enchanted Mesa) near Acoma Pueblo, ca. 1932.
Photo by Witter Bynner. *(MNM 92161)*

❖ ❖ ❖

Detail of wall painting, Kuaua Pueblo ruins. *(MNM 31074)*

❖ ❖ ❖

Taos Pueblo, the northernmost pueblo in the Rio Grande valley.
Photo by William Henry Jackson. *(MNM 4510)*

CHAPTER 2
Conquistadores and Faith

Spain sought wealth and souls. Of the two, the second quickly became the prime factor in the exploration of New Mexico. After Vásquez de Coronado the dreams of material grandeur died for that land to the north. But the enticement of taking the faith to a pagan people, especially if they lived in villages, became incentive enough for further exploration and eventual settlement. In the process, Spaniards would penetrate through New Mexico into the heart of the North American continent. They learned of new people, places, and things that forever changed them.

He [Viceroy Mendoza] reminded them of the allegiance they owed their general, explaining to them the benefits that might result from carrying out the expedition, not only for the conversion of the natives, but for those who conquered the land, and for the service of his Majesty; and he reminded them of the obligation that the king had assumed to help and favor them at all times. This finished, he received, upon the gospels in a missal, the oaths of all in general, both leaders and soldiers, all in proper order. They swore that they would follow their general and would obey and do on that expedition all that was commanded them. This they afterward fulfilled faithfully, as will be shown. After this, on the following day, the army set out with flags unfurled.[1]

— *On the Coronado expedition (1540–1542), Pedro de Castañeda de Nájera, 1560*

❖ ❖ ❖

Capt. Gen. Hernán Cortés, conquerer and governor of Mexico. Detail from an
anonymous painting done around one hundred years after his death and copied
from an original. Hospital de Jesus, Mexico City. *(MNM 112517)*

There had gathered for this expedition the most brilliant company ever assembled in the Indies to go in search of new lands.[2]

— *On the Coronado expedition, Pedro de Castañeda de Nájera, 1560*

As he [Coronado] stood out among all the others because of his gilded armor and some plumes in his helmet, all the Indians shot at him, as a marked man.[3]

— *On the Coronado expedition at Zuni Pueblo, García López de Cárdenez, 1540*

There [Zuni] we found something we prized more than gold or silver, namely much maize, beans, and chickens larger than those here of New Spain [Mexico], and salt better and whiter than I have ever seen in my whole life.[4]

— *On the Coronado expedition, García López de Cárdenez, 1540*

Cicuye [Pecos] is a pueblo containing about 500 warriors. It is feared throughout that land. It is square, perched on a rock in the center of a vast patio or plaza, with its *estufas* [kivas]. The houses are all alike, four stories high. One can walk on the roofs over the whole pueblo, there being no streets to prevent this. The second terrace is all surrounded with lanes which enable one to circle the whole pueblo. These lanes are like balconies which project out, and under which one may find shelter. The houses have no doors on the ground floor. The inhabitants use movable ladders to climb to the corridors, which are on the inner side of the pueblos. They enter them that way, as the doors of the houses open into the corridors on this terrace. The corridors are used as streets. The houses facing the open country are back to back with those on the patio, and in time of war they are entered through the interior ones. The pueblo is surrounded by a low stone wall. Inside there is a water spring, which can be diverted from them. The people of this town pride themselves because no one has been able to subjugate them, while they dominate the pueblos they wish. The inhabitants [of Cicuye] are of the same type and have the same customs as those in the other pueblos. The maidens

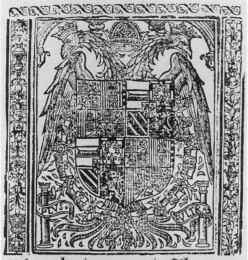

❖ ❖ ❖

Coat of Arms of Spain. Page from the original edition of *Relación y comentarios* of Alvar Núñez Cabeza de Vaca. Published in Valladolid in 1555. From *The Spanish Southwest* (Albuquerque: The Quivíra Society, 1937). *(MNM 152695)*
Buffalo as pictured in Francisco López de Gómara's *Historia general de las Indias,* 1554. *(MNM 152668)*

here also go about naked until they take a husband. For they say that if they do anything wrong it will soon be noticed and so they will not do it.[5]

— On the Coronado expedition, Pedro de Castañeda de Nájera, 1560

Over these plains roam natives following the cattle, hunting and dressing skins to take to the pueblos to sell in winter there, each group to the nearest place. Some go to the pueblos of Cicuye, others to Quivira, and others toward Florida to the settlements located in the direction of that region and port. . . . From what was seen of these natives and of others which they said lived in other sections, they are by far more numerous than those of the pueblos, better proportioned, greater warriors, and more feared. They go about like nomads with their tents and with packs of dogs harnessed with little pads, pack-saddles, and girths. When the dogs' loads slip to the side they howl for someone to come and straighten them.[6]

— On the Coronado expedition, Pedro de Castañeda de Nájera, 1560

After weighing and deliberating upon the obstacles and difficulties that would be encountered in an undertaking of such magnitude, we determined, together with seven other companions with whom we discussed the enter-prise, to carry out the said expedition, which had for its ultimate object the service of God our Lord, the preaching of His law and gospel to all men, and the extension of the dominions of the royal crown of Castile.

After discussing the matter with some friars of the Franciscan order who gladly offered to go on the expedition, and having obtained in advance the permission and authority of your Excellency, we set out. We were three Franciscan friars and nine soldiers, provided with arms and horses at our own cost.[7]

— On the Rodríquez-Chamuscado expedition, Hernán Gallegos, 1582

We continued in the direction the Indians had indicated to us on the previous day, taking along guides who led us to the river of which they had told us at that time. This river formed a valley, the best and most pleasing that

❖ ❖ ❖

Spanish colonial spur excavated at Pecos Pueblo, ca. 1600.
Collections of the Museum of International Folk Art. *(MNM 152910)*

we had seen on the trip; we named it *Nuestra Señora de la Concepción* [now the Rio Grande].[8]

— On the Rodríguez-Chamuscado expedition, Hernán Gallegos, 1582

These people [Indians in the El Paso area] accompanied us at night and performed dances for us. Their nation has a rhythm in its dances, resembling that of Negroes, produced by beating some skins attached to a vessel in the fashion of a tambourine. After doing this, the dancers rise, execute their movements, revolving to the rhythm of the music like clowns. They raise their hands toward the sun and sing in their language, with the cadence of the dance, "ayia canima." This they do with much unity and harmony, in such a way that though there are three hundred savages in a dance, it seems as if it were being sung and danced by one man only, due to the fine harmony and measure of their performance.[9]

— On the Rodríguez-Chamuscado expedition, Hernán Gallegos, 1582

You know that the main purposes of your journey are these: to put a stop to the expedition planned and undertaken by Gaspar Castaño [de Sosa] and his men in contravention of my specific order as well as the general orders of his Majesty; to check the injuries and excesses against the poor natives which have done such great disservice to God our Lord and his Majesty; and to insure the punishment of those who perpetrated the offenses, as well as giving satisfaction to the Indians for abuses already suffered and assurance that they will not be so abused in the future but will receive only wholehearted friendship and good treatment.[10]

— On the purpose of his expedition, Viceroy Don Luis de Velasco to Juan Morlete, 1590

Since it is fitting that such disobedience and impudence be punished, I hereby command you to bring to trial the aforesaid Gaspar Castaño [de Sosa], with the other culprits, and to proceed against them in accordance with the law. Furthermore, you shall neither encourage nor permit the enslavement of

DI RFANCESCO VAZQVEZ

regni ch'io dico, all'hora si potria meglio vedere senza metter à pericolo la mia persona, & D
lassar per questo di dar relation delle cose vedute. solamente viddi dalla bocca della campagna sette villaggi ragioneuoli, alquato lontani, in vna valle di sotto molto fresca & di molto
buona terra, donde vsciuano molti fiumi, hebbi informatiõe che in qlla era molto oro, et che
gli habitatori l'adoperano in vasi & palettine, con lequali si radono & leuano via il sudore, &
che sono gente che non consentono che quelli d'altra parte della campagna contrattino con
loro, & non mi seppero dir la causa. Qui posi due croci, & tolsi il possesso di tutta la campagna & valle per la maniera & ordine delli possessi tolti da me di sopra conforme alla instrut-
tione, & di li prosegui il ritorno del mio viaggio con la maggior pressa ch'io potei fin ch'io
arriuai alla terra di san Michiele della prouincia di Culiacan, credendo trouar in quel luogo
Francesco Vazquez di Coronado Gouernator della nuoua Galitia, & non trouandolo pro
segui il mio cammino fino alla città di Compostella doue lo trouai. Non scriuo qui molte altre particolarità, perche non sono pertinenti à questo caso. solamente dico quello ch'io viddi, & mi fu detto delle terre per doue andai, & di quelle che hebbi informatione.

RELATIONE CHE MANDO' FRANCESCO
Vazquez di Coronado, Capitano Generale della gente che fu mandata
in nome di Sua Maesta al paese nouamente scoperto, quel che
successe nel viaggio dalli ventidua d'Aprile di questo anno E
M D X L, che parti da Culiacan per innanzi, & di quel che
trouo nel paese doue andaua.

*Francesco Vazquez con essercito parte di Culiacan, et doppo il patire diuersi incommodi nel mal viag
gio, gionge alla Valle de i Caraconi, la ritroua sterile di Maiz: per hauerne, manda nella Valle
detta del Signore, ha relatione della grandezza della Valle di Caraconi, & di
quelli popoli, & di alcune Isole poste in quelle costiere.*

Lli ventiduoi del Mese d'Aprile passato, parti dalla prouincia di Culiacan
con parte dell'essercito & con l'ordine che io scrissi à V.S. & secondo il suc-
cesso tengo per certo che si in douino à non metter tutto l'essercito vnito in
questa impresa, perche sono stati cosi grandi i trauagli & mancamento della
vettouaglia che credo che in tutto questo anno non si potesse effettuar la
impresa, et gia che si effettuasse sarebbe con gran perdita di gente, perche co
me scrissi à V.S. io feci il viaggio di Culiacan in ottanta giorni di strada la
quale, io & quei gentil'huomini à cauallo miei compagni portãmo su le spalle & ne nostri ca
ualli, vn poco di vettouaglia, in modo che da questa impoi nõ portammo niun di noi d'altre F
robbe necessarie tanto che passasse vna libra, & con tutto cio, & con l'essersi messa in questa
poca vettouaglia che portammo tutta quella regola & ordine possibile, ci mancò, & non è
da farsene marauiglia, perche il camino e aspro & lungo, & fra gli archibusi che si portauano
nel sallir delle montagne & coste, & nel passar de i fiumi ci si guasto la maggior parte del
Maiz: & perche io mando à V.S. dipinto questo viaggio nõ le diro in cio altro per qsta mia.
Trenta leghe prima che si arriuasse al luogo che il padre Prouinciale nella sua relatione
cosi ben diceua, mandai Melchior Diaz con quindici da cauallo innanzi, ordinandogli che
facesse di due giornate vna, accioche hauessi esaminato il tutto quando io giongessi: ilqua-
le, camminò quattro giorni per certe montagne asprissime, et non trouò quiui ne da viuere,
ne gẽte, ne information di alcuna cosa, eccetto che trouò due ò tre pouere villette, di venti
ò trenta capanne l'una, & da gli habitatori di essa seppe che da li auanti non si trouaua se non
asprissime montagne che continouauano, disabitate da tutte le genti, & perche era cosa per-
duta non volsi di qui mandar di cio messo à V.S. diedi dispiacere à tutti i compagni, che vna
cosa tanto lodata, & di che il padre haueua detto tante cose si fosse trouato tanto al contra-
rio, & si fece giudicio che il rimanente fosse tutto di quella sorte. Et veduto io questo procu-
rai di rallegrargli al meglio che io potei, dicendogli che V.S. sempre hebbe oppinione che
questo viaggio fosse vna cosa gittata via, & che douessimo metter il nostro pẽsiero in quelle
sette

Chapter heading for the first published account of Francisco Vásquez de Coronado's 1540–
1541 expedition into New Mexico and present-day Kansas. From "Relatione Che Mando
Francesco di Coronado . . . ," in Giovanni Batista Ramusio, *Navigationi et viaggi . . . ,*
published in Venice in 1556. Original copy in History Library, Palace of the Governors.
(MNM 152669)

NEW MEXICO.
Otherwise,
The Voiage of Anthony of
ESPEIO, who in the yeare 1583. with
his company, discouered a Lande of 15.
Prouinces, replenished with Townes and villages, with houses of 4. or 5. stories height,
It lieth Northward, and some suppose
that the same way men may by places inhabited go to the Lande
tearmed De Labrador.

Translated out of the Spanish copie printed first at Madreol, 1586, and afterward
at Paris, in the same yeare.

Imprinted at London for
Thomas Cadman.

❖ ❖ ❖

English translation of Antonio de Espejo's narrative, published in 1587. From Wagner,
The Spanish Southwest, 1937. *(MNM 152670)*

any Indians whatsoever, and if you hear of any who have been made slaves you shall set them free.[11]

— Phillip II, the King of Spain, to the Audiencia of New Spain, January 17, 1593

The charges against the defendant were invasion of lands inhabited by peaceable Indians, raising troops, entry into the provinces of New Mexico. . . . We find that, by reason of the guilt proved against the said Captain Gaspar Castaño in these proceedings, we should and do condemn him to exactly six years of exile from the jurisdiction of New Spain, during which period he shall serve his Majesty in the Philippine Islands.[12]

— Sentence imposed on Castaño de Sosa, March 5, 1593

CHAPTER 3

The Spanish Colonial Period

Settlement came in 1598. Not unlike the English colonies of the United States, the early Spanish colony had to learn some hard lessons in survival. New Mexico was the only true landlocked colony established in the Americas during this period. All other colonies — Spanish, English, French, Dutch, and Portuguese — had quick and easy access to water transportation. And there was another difference. Even with the successful Pueblo Indian Revolt, New Mexico's Indians fared better with the early Spanish colonists than did the Indians on the East Coast with English colonists.

And, since Don Luis de Velasco, my viceroy, has discussed and contracted with you, Don Juan de Oñate, concerning this project, and you have accepted it with the conditions and stipulations which will be delivered to you, signed and attested by a notary, therefore, in conformity with them and the ordinances which relate to new discoveries and pacifications, I order them delivered to you so that you may keep and observe them; and, since I approve and ratify the said capitulations, as I do, I give the contract my approval. Therefore trusting in you and that you will carry out this discovery and pacification in a Christian spirit and with complete loyalty, in the form and manner set forth in the contract, I appoint you as my governor, captain general, *caudillo,* discoverer, and pacifier of the said provinces of New Mexico and those adjacent and

41

neighboring, in order that, in my royal name, you may enter them with the settlers and armed forces, baggage, equipment, munitions, and other necessary things that you may provide for the purpose. You will endeavor to attract the natives with peace, friendship, and good treatment, which I particularly charge you, and to induce them to hear and accept the holy gospel; you will explain our holy Catholic faith to them through interpreters, if they can be obtained, so that we may have communication with them in the various languages and seek their conversations; let it be done at the opportunity which the friars find most suitable. You will see to it that the latter are respected and revered, as ministers of the gospel should be, so that, with this example, the Indians may attend and honor them and accept their persuasions and teachings. Experience has demonstrated this to be very important, and also that all the people in your company act gently and kindly, without committing excesses or setting bad examples, or irritating those we seek to attract lest they adopt an unfriendly attitude toward the faith. You are to direct everything to this principal aim, which is, as you see, a matter of importance, arrange all details with good sense and judgement to the service of God and the increase of our Holy Catholic faith.[13]

— Appointment of Don Juan de Oñate
as governor and captain general of New Mexico,
King Felipe II, October 21, 1595

If in the said provinces, any seaports should be found on the North Sea which might be utilized without the harmful results that either by becoming infested with enemies and by opening a gate through which the profits might be lost, as soon as any such harbor is discovered, you shall notify the viceroy of New Spain, telling him the news and giving an accurate report of the configuration of the coast and the capacity of each harbor, in order that he may take suitable measures. Until this is done you are not to make use of these harbors or consent to anyone's doing so.[14]

— Viceroy Luis de Velasco to Governor Don Juan de Oñate,
instructions of October 21, 1595

❖ ❖ ❖

Gaspar Pérez de Villagrá, age fifty-five, from the original edition of *Historia de la Nueva Mexico,* published in Alcala, Spain, in 1610. Original edition in History Library, Palace of the Governors. *(MNM 152680)*
Petroglyph of a Spanish rider, Cienega. Photo ca. 1925–1930. *(MNM 42435)*

Because we are zealous of our honor and sign complaints, we are labeled as traitors. The fact is that we are all depressed, cowed, and frightened, expecting death at any moment. We are not masters of ourselves or of our children. We find ourselves in the most harrowing position of servitude ever endured by Spaniards, and threatened with the loss of our rights. Who can help but complain about matters here, being unfortunate subjects of your lordship? We had all come so eagerly to serve you in this conversion at our own expense, but, after spending many thousands from our estates, we did not have the fortune to be governed by a person such as you, but instead by one whose treatment is such that unless his majesty sends relief, we shall doubtless all perish with our women and children.[15]

— *Captain Luis Gasco de Velasco to the viceroy, March 22, 1601*

The Council of the Indies has studied what you tell me in a letter of March 7 of this year in regard to the present state of the *entrada* and discovery of New Mexico, the scanty harvest of souls that has been reaped thus far and that may be expected in the future, the difficulties or insurmountable obstacles and excessive cost in preserving or extending it, and the little benefit that the land offers both to my royal treasury and to those who settle there, because of its limitations and poverty and other matters which you set forth.

. . . upon consultation, it has seemed fitting to order you, as I do order and command, that you order the suspension of the discovery and exploration of New Mexico.[16]

— *Phillip III, the King of Spain, to his viceroy, September 13, 1608*

The sergeant and his men then went forth into the plain where they saw immense herds of these cattle. They are about the size of a Castilian bull, extremely wooly, hump-backed, black-horned, and have splendid meat. They yield great amounts of lard and tallow. They have beards like billy-goats, and are as fleet of foot as deer. They go together in great herds of as many as twenty or thirty thousand.[17]

— *Gaspar Pérez de Villagrá, describing the American bison, 1610*

44

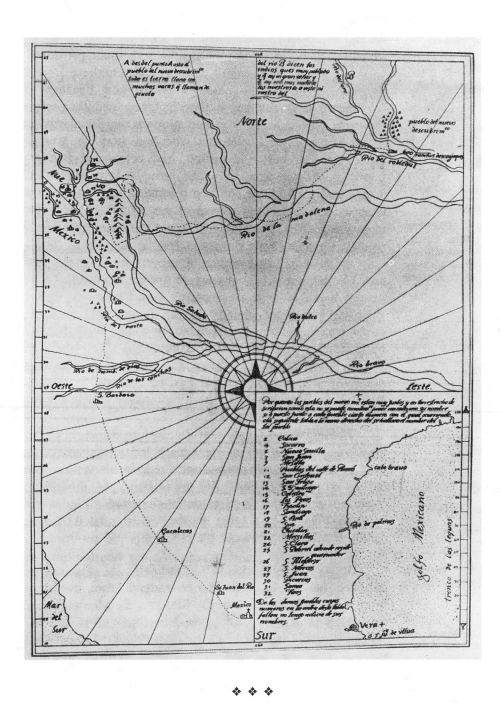

Enrique Martínez's sketch map of New Mexico, ca. 1602, reflecting Oñate's exploration of the plains. The Pueblo de los Pecos in no. 16. Courtesy of the Archivo General de Indias, Seville, Spain. *(MNM 108663)*

It is understood that that country [New Mexico] is settled by various languages very difficult and barbarous which cause many inconveniences for the good administration and consolation of the ministers as well as of the natives. The said Governor is requested to act with great care consulting with the religious in such a manner so that the main thing shall be to teach all the Indians and especially the children and ignorant persons so they may learn the Spanish language and in the event that they cannot learn the same generally an effort must at least be made that those who have no natural fitness to learn the Spanish language must be taught the language most generally spoken in that country so that they may be better administrated.[18]

— Viceroy Don Luis de Velasco to Governor Pedro de Peralta, 1609

[B]ecause it is most necessary to look to the conservation, comfort and good treatment of the said Indians: I command you that the allotting which you may have to make of them be only that of tilling and herding and for no other purpose, and even this you shall make from the pueblos that which may be convenient to it so that the Indians be not molested, and the number that you may have to apportion shall be at the ration of two percent of those who may be in each pueblo in ordinary time, which is when they are not sowing or reaping, and in time of double [work] when there is the said reaping and sowing you shall make the said apportionment at the rate of eight percent, giving orders that the said Indians be paid one *real* for each day; and you shall take great care that good treatment be done them, and to those Spaniards who may not so do nor pay them for their work you shall not allow any more Distribution of Indians from that time forth.[19]

— Don Diego Fernández de Córdova, Marqués de Guadalcazar,
to Governor Don Juan de Eulate, regarding Indian labor, July 29, 1620

For this blessed province of the Holy Gospel has, as it has always had, religious of very great spirit who desire to go among those infidel and barbarous nations, to lay down their lives among them, in imitation of the One who for our love gave up his life on the tree of the cross.[20]

— Fray Gerónimo de Zárate Salmerón, 1626

46

❖ ❖ ❖

Ruins of Quarai Pueblo mission church, ca. 1940. Photo by Hector de Castro.
(MNM 58328)

❖ ❖ ❖

Arched doorway, Pecos Pueblo mission church ruins, ca. 1915.
Photo probably by Jesse L. Nusbaum. *(MNM 12925)*

❖ ❖ ❖

Ruins of mission church of San José de las Jémez, Guisewa Pueblo, ca. 1922.
Photo by Wesley Bradfield. *(MNM 12891)*

❖ ❖ ❖

Mission church, Zía Pueblo, built ca. 1614. Photo by Odd Halseth, 1923. *(MNM 4866)*

I, Fray Alonso de Benavides of the Order of St. Francis, Custodian of the Missions and Custody of New Mexico, declare that the events and affairs of that kingdom or, better said, of that new world, which during these recent years we friars of my father St. Francis have converted and pacified unto God our Lord and brought under obedience to Your Majesty, are so numerous and of such a nature that I shall find it impossible to describe them at one hearing and in a summary manner. The reason is that, with the royal assistance and protection of Your Majesty, we have discovered such great treasures, both spiritual and temporal, which the divine Majesty has seen fit to confirm with so many wonders and miracles, that the Viceroy of Mexico and my order thought it best to instruct me, as the one who has for many years governed and administered that country, to come in person to describe and represent them to Your Majesty.[21]

— *Fray Alonso de Benavides, 1630*

But today, after so few years, all that region is covered with churches and with crosses set on pedestals, and its inhabitants greet one another aloud in words of praise for the Most Blessed Sacrament of the Altar for the Most Holy Name of Jesus Christ.

God left it and entrusted it to Your Majesty, so that through these Catholic means and through your royal expenditures you might enjoy many spiritual and temporal blessings.[22]

— *Fray Alonso de Benavides, 1630*

The weather is of either extreme, for in the winter it is very severe, with so much snow, ice and cold that all the rivers, *esteros* and even the Rio del Norte freeze so hard that loaded wagons pass over them, and immense herds race across them as if over dry land . . . for since the rivers are frozen, they have a glassy and slippery surface that occasions terrible falls whether one be traveling on horseback or on foot. The remedy for this is to scatter some earth on top, so that a good foothold can be obtained. But it is impossible to find any earth, because everything is frozen so hard that even to dig a grave at the church a fire must first be kindled on top of the ground in order to thaw it. . . .

❖ ❖ ❖

Cross at sunset, Pecos Pueblo, ca. 1912. Photo by Jesse L. Nusbaum. *(MNM 12929)*

❖ ❖ ❖

View across Pecos Valley toward Pecos Pueblo mission ruins, 1915.
Photo by Jesse L. Nusbaum. *(MNM 12944)*

Every winter a great number of Indians out in the country are frozen, and many Spaniards have their ears, feet and hands frozen.[23]

— Fray Alonso de Benavides, 1630

We asked the Indians why they were so zealous in asking for Baptism and for friars to go to instruct them in Christian doctrine. They replied that a woman, similar to the one whose likeness we had there painted, used to tell them, each in his own language, to come without delay and summon the priests that they might teach and baptize them.[24]

— Fray Alonso de Benavides, describing Indian sightings of María de Agreda, 1630

At dawn the holy woman spoke to each one of them separately and told them not to leave, because the friars they had sent for were already drawing near.[25]

— Fray Alonso de Benavides, describing Indian sightings of María de Agreda, 1630

These people [the Pueblos] have always had a government and republic, the old men assembling with the chief captain to deliberate and to decide what things were most desirable for them.[26]

— Fray Alonso de Benavides, 1630

The natives are very fond of them [the friars] and of things pertaining to the church, which they attend with extraordinary love and devotion.

Ample evidence of this is their many churches and friaries, all built by the women and by boys and girls taking Christian doctrine, although this may seem an exaggeration since these structures are so sumptuous and ornate. It is the custom among these nations for the women to build the houses, while the men spin, weave blankets, go to war and do the hunting; and if we compel any man to work on building a house, he runs away and the women laugh at him. In this way, there have been erected more than fifty churches, whose ceilings are attractively carved with interlaced flowers, and whose walls are

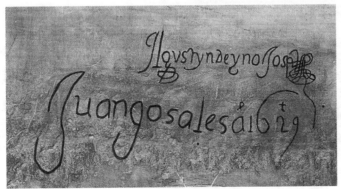

❖ ❖ ❖

Sixteenth-century Franciscan monk of New Mexico, from *Atzlán: The History, Resources and Attractions of New Mexico* by William G. Ritch, 1885. *(MNM 87294)*
Spanish inscriptions left at El Morro by Agustín de Ynojos and Juan Gonzales in 1629.
Photo by George Grant, 1934. *(MNM 57377)*

very well painted. This is possible because of the wonderful mountains containing every kind of wood, and also because we friars have taken such pains in training the Indians of the *doctrina* that there can be found among them skilled carpenters and craftsmen of every kind.[27]

— *Fray Alonso de Benavides, 1630*

In the course of the year that I have unworthily served as guardian of this convent, I have not seen the said governor or any minister of justice punish any fornicator, idolator, or sorcerer in this pueblo; what I have seen is that they [the officials] punish them [the Indians] because they do not bring in salt, because they do not promptly cut wood.[28]

— *Fray Nicolás de Freitas, June 18, 1660*

To this the said General Don Diego de Peñalosa replied: "If the custodian excommunicated me, I would hang him or garrot him immediately, and if the Pontiff came here and wanted to excommunicate me or actually did so, I would hang the Pontiff, because in this kingdom, I am the prince and the supreme magistrate."[29]

— *Fray Alonso de Posada, May 16, 1664*

Six years before [the 1680 Pueblo Indian Revolt], a girl of ten, the daughter of the High Sheriff, and who was in great pains, commended herself in her paralysis to an Image of N.S. del Sagrario which she had before her. Instantly she found herself cured. And in describing the miracle with wonder, she said that the Virgin had told her: "Child, arise and announce that this Custody will soon see itself destroyed because of the poor regard that it has for my Priests, the people must make amends for the fault if they do not wish to undergo the punishment."[30]

— *On the miraculous prediction of the 1680 Pueblo Indian Revolt, made by a statue of the Virgin that became known as Our Lady of the Macana, Fray Agustín Vetancurt, 1698, in* Theatro Mexicano, *4th part, treatise 3, number 64*

56

❖ ❖ ❖

Title page of Fray Alonso de Benavides's *Memorial,* originally published in Madrid in 1630. From the Ayer edition of 1916. *(MNM 152681)*
María de Jesús de Agreda, the Lady in Blue. From Benavides's *Revised Memorial,* published in Madrid in 1634. *(MNM 152682)*

❖ ❖ ❖

Nuestra Señora de la Macana, the statue that miraculously predicted the 1680 Pueblo Indian
Revolt to a young girl. The statue is in the Convento de San Francisco in Mexico City.
From *The Lady from Toledo* by Fray Angelico Chávez, 1960. *(MNM 152683)*

Before entering upon this government I received information of the general uprising of the Indians of the provinces of New Mexico. According to the *autos* [official hearings], reports, and documents which were remitted to this government, on the thirteenth day of August of the past year 1680 the rebellious Indians, by prearranged conspiracy, fell upon all the pueblos and farms at the same time with such vigor and cruelty that they killed twenty-one missionary religious — nineteen priests and two lay brothers — and more than three hundred Spaniards, not sparing the defenselessness of the women and children.[31]

— *Viceroy Marqués de la Laguna, February 28, 1681*

I asked him [Pueblo leader Luis Picurí, also known as Tupatu of Picurís Pueblo] to enter the said tent, where affectionate words were showered upon him and where he was served chocolate, which he drank with the fathers, with me, and with others present.[32]

— *Governor Don Diego de Vargas, journal entry, September 15, 1692*

The Pueblos and people who would not believe and obey me and carry out all that which I told them, and which his majesty, the King, our Lord, ordered them, those I would consume immediately; and that for this reason the others who had obeyed me and rendered obedience should not change their minds, for all those who were good I would hold near to my heart and esteem greatly.[33]

— *Governor Don Diego de Vargas, journal entry, September 16, 1692*

It is my wish that with those with whom I enter, that they should first and foremost, personally build the Church and holy temple, setting up in it before all else the patroness of the Kingdom and Villa, who is the one that was saved from the ferocity of the savages, her title being Our Lady of the Conquest.[34]

— *Governor Don Diego de Vargas to Viceroy Conde de Galve, El Paso, January 2, 1693*

❖ ❖ ❖

Diego José López de Zárate Vargas Pimentel Zapata y Luján Ponce de León Cepeda Alvarez
Contreras y Salinas, Marqués de Villanueva de la Sagra y de la Nava de Braciñas
(1643–1704), captain general of New Mexico and twice governor of New Mexico
(1691–1697, 1703–1704), from a painting. *(MNM 11409)*

Title page from Carlos de Sigüenza y Góngora's *Mercurio Volante,* published as a tribute to
Diego de Vargas on the occasion of his "reconquest" of New Mexico in 1692.
From *The Spanish Southwest,* 1937. *(MNM 152671)*
Spanish document signed by Diego de Vargas in 1696. *(HSNM/MNM 15035)*

61

❖ ❖ ❖

Detail of *Segesser II*, an early eighteenth-century hide painting of the ambush of the 1720
Pedro de Villasur expedition. Collections of the Palace of the Governors. *(MNM 152690)*
Detail of *Segesser II*. Villasur lies dead in the foreground. Collections of the Palace of
the Governors. *(MNM 152909)*

It is the saddest, the most lamentable, and the most fatal event that has happened in New Mexico since the time of its conquest. . . . in the villa of Santa Fe, thirty-two widows and many orphaned children, whose tears reach the sky, mourn the poor ability of the governor; pray God for his punishment, and await the remedy of your justice.[35]

— Former Governor of New Mexico Felipe Martínez to Viceroy Baltasar de Zuñiga,
Marqués de Valero, Duque de Arion, Mexico City, October 8, 1720

In detail he refers to the third day of November of the year just passed, when more than three hundred Comanches attacked the pueblo of Galisteo, notwithstanding that during the previous month of July, they had been admitted and entertained by the governor in the pueblo of Taos. There they held and participated in the fair, where they are accustomed to ransom their kinsmen for hides.[36]

— Marqués de Altamira to Governor Thomás Vélez Gachupín, April 26, 1752

I am enclosing the printed Franciscan almanac which they [the Navajos] brought. When you understand the reason, your lordship will have sufficient cause to appreciate the fine strategy of the Navajo Apaches and to laud the worthy actions of friendship of the Utes. The case is as follows: The Utes attacked the Peñoles of the Navajos with such force that the Apaches found the action bloody for them; some were killed, others captured, with no danger to the Utes, who strove for a complete victory by closing in to reach the top of the mesa. Then the Apaches came out, after stacking their arms, carrying a wooden cross above which was this said almanac on a pole. They told the Utes: "The great chief of the Spaniards sent you this letter and the cross and ordered you to be our friends." Thereupon those who before were lions became lambs, surrendered their arms, and received the cross and the false letter. The chiefs held their conference there and agreed that since your lordship punished the Comanches severely and after pardoned them benignly when they sought peace by carrying another similar cross, it was but proper that they should do the same, both to imitate their action and not to displease your lordship, who, if angered by their ignoring your letter, might take up arms against them.[37]

— Juan Joseph Lobato to Governor Thomás Vélez Gachupín, August 17, 1752

63

Most excellent Sir [the Viceroy]: On the 6th of August last, two French traders arrived at the pueblo of Pecos from the province of Canada or New France, which lies to the north-northeast of this Kingdom of New Mexico. . . . As soon as I learned of it from the reverend father missionary by letter, I ordered the *alcalde mayor* of those pueblos, who at the moment was in this villa, to go at once to Pecos, arrest the two Frenchmen, seize the goods they were carrying, and bring the men in person to this villa [Santa Fe].

After this was done, I proceeded to examine them as far as the limited understanding of the interpreter, the only one in this region, permitted. Through him I learned . . . that, with permission of the commander of the *presidio* of Illinois, they set out under orders to discover this kingdom and to inform themselves of the route and the distance. They brought with them a small quantity of goods to test whether this government would permit the opening of trade with that of Canada. . . . They showed themselves unaware of the prohibition against free trade as well as of the arrival in the past year of the four Frenchmen from New Orleans with the same purpose.[38]

— *Governor Thomás Vélez Gachupín to Conde de Revilla Gijedo, September 18, 1752*

For about thirty years the governors have collected the tithes; all the tithes from down the river are collected in the Villa of Albuquerque (a Spanish villa), the *alcalde mayor* of which has the duty of receiving them. The Indians haul them gratis, and at the proper time take their own in wagons to the Villa of Santa Fe.[39]

— *Fray Juan Sanz de Lezaún, 1760*

On May 29, 1760, I went to the pueblo of the Pecos Indians. . . . I finished my visitation of that kingdom and I left for the outside world in July. During the month of September those Indians of Pecos arranged a function similar to my reception and to other ceremonies I celebrated there. The originator of this performance was one of the Indian principal men of that pueblo. . . . He made himself a bishop, and, in order to present himself to his people as such, he designed and cut pontifical vestments. . . .

❖ ❖ ❖

Early nineteenth-century *adarga,* or bullhide shield. Collections of the Historical
Society of New Mexico/Museum of International Folk Art HSNM/MOIFA. *(MNM 148100)*
Chimayó with its Plaza del Cerro, built in 1730. Photo by Haddon-Branham, ca. 1960.
(MNM 59316)

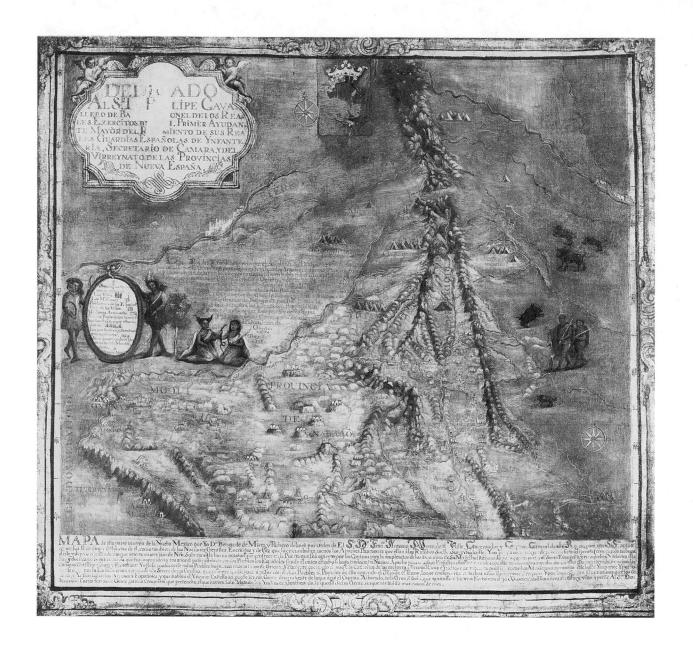

❖ ❖ ❖

Map of New Mexico by Don Bernardo de Miera y Pacheo, 1740–1756. Oil on canvass original.
Collections of the Palace of the Governors.

Interior of the church at Las Trampas constructed around 1760.
Photo by Jesse L. Nusbaum, ca. 1912. *(MNM 14165)*

❖ ❖ ❖

Section from the 1761 stone reredos from La Castrense Military Chapel,
which was built on the south side of Santa Fe's plaza in the same year.
Photo by Jesse L. Nusbaum, ca. 1912. *(MNM 61352)*

The aforesaid . . . donned all of this, mounted an ass, and two other Indians got themselves up to accompany him in the capacity of assistants. One took the part of the Father Custos [Custodian]. They put a garment like the Franciscan habit on him, and they painted the other black to represent my man. These two also rode similar mounts, and, after all the Indian population had assembled along with others who were not Indians, to the accompaniment of a muffled drum and loud huzzas, the whole crew . . . departed for the pueblo. . . . They went straight to the plaza, where the Indian women were kneeling in two rows. And . . . the make-believe bishop went between them distributing blessings . . . They proceeded to the place where they had prepared a great arbor with two seats in it. Agustín, who was playing the part of the bishop, occupied the chief one, and Mateo Cruz, who was acting the Custos, the other.

And the latter immediately rose and informed the crowd in a loud voice that the bishop ordered them to approach and be confirmed. They promptly obeyed, and Agustín . . . used the following method of confirming each one who came to him: He made a cross on his forehead with water, and when he gave him a buffet, that one left and the next one came forward. In this occupation he spent all the time necessary to dispatch his people, and after the confirmations were over, the meal which had been prepared for the occasion was served. Then the dance with which they completed the afternoon followed. On the next day the diversion and festivities continued, beginning with a mass which Bishop Agustín pretended to say in the same arbor. During it he distributed pieces of tortilla made of wheat flour in imitation of communion. And the rest of the day the amusement was dancing, and the same continued on the third day which brought those disorders and entertainments to an end.[40]

— *Bishop Pedro Tamarón y Romeral, 1760*

Some poor men whom the governors install as *alcaldes mayores,* individuals who have not prospered in other office or who have been ruined in trade; or deserters from studies by which they did not profit, who became paper shufflers and swindlers. Such are usually the qualifications of these *alcaldes mayores,* a career aspired to by useless or ruined men.[41]

— *Bishop Pedro Tamarón y Romeral, 1760*

n 24

RELACION

DEL ATENTADO SACRILEGIO,

COMETIDO POR TRES INDIOS

1760 DE UN PUEBLO

DE LA PROVINCIA

DEL NUEVO MEXICO;

Y DE EL SEVERO CASTIGO,

QUE EXECUTÒ

LA DIVINA JUSTICIA

CCN EL FAUTOR PRINCIPAL

DE ELLOS.

Impreſſa, con las licencias neceſſarias,
en Mexico en la Imprenta de la Bi-
bliotheca Mexicana, en la Puente del
Eſpiritu Santo. Año de 1763.

❖ ❖ ❖

Title page of Bishop Pedro Tamarón y Romeral's six-page "Narrative of the Attempted
Sacrilege Committed by Three Indians of a Pueblo of the Province of New Mexico and the
Severe Punishment Divine Retribution Inflicted Upon the Main Perpetrator Among Them,"
published in Mexico City in 1763. From Wagner, *The Spanish Southwest,* 1937.
(MNM 152672)
Metal cross excavated at Saint Francis Cathedral in Santa Fe. Photo taken in 1966.
(MNM 47984)

It [Santa Fe] was founded in 1682 [sic], at the foot of a high mountain range from which flows a crystal clear river full of small but choice trout. The river comes from a lake, supplied by numerous springs, at the summit of the mountain and flows through the center of the town. The climate is like that of the two Castiles; it has its season of snow and rain, it is mild in spring, and extremely hot in summer.[42]

— *Don Pedro Alonso O'Crowley, 1774*

There are also little orchards with vinestocks and small apricot, peach, apple, and pear trees. Delicious melons and watermelons are grown. Not all those who have grapes make wine, but some do. The citizens are of all classes and walks of life as in the other places I have mentioned, and they speak the local Spanish.[43]

— *On Albuquerque, Fray Francisco Atanasio Domínguez, 1776*

Every year, between the end of October and the beginning of November many heathens of the Ute nation come to the vicinity of this pueblo [Abiquiu]. They come very well laden with good deerskins, and they celebrate their fair with them. This is held for the sole purpose of buying horses. If one is much to the taste and satisfaction of an Indian, he gives fifteen to twenty good deerskins for the horse; and if not, there is no purchase. They also sell deer or buffalo meat for maize or corn flour.[44]

— *On Abiquiu, Fray Francisco Atanasio Domínguez, 1776*

The villa itself consists of twenty-four houses near the mission. The rest of what is called Albuquerque extends upstream to the north, and all of it is a settlement of ranchos on the meadows of the said river [Rio del Norte] for the distance of a league from the church to the last one upstream.[45]

— *Fray Francisco Atanasio Domínguez, 1776*

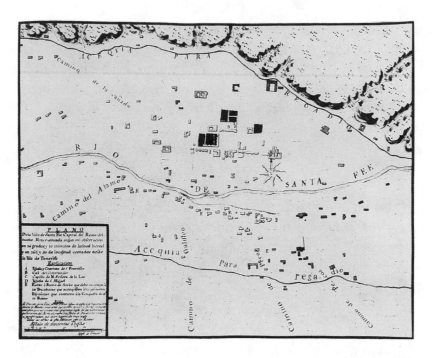

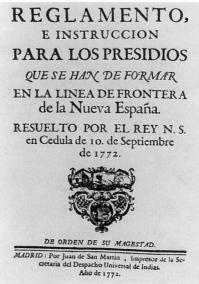

❖ ❖ ❖

José de Urrutia's map of Santa Fe, 1766. Original in the British Library. (*MNM 15048*)
Title page of the *Reglamento* governing the frontier military, published in Madrid in 1772.
From *The Spanish Southwest,* 1937. (*MNM 152673*)

Map of the Interior Province of New Mexico, which Don Bernardo de Miera y Pacheco, exempt soldier of the Royal Presidio of Santa Fe, made by order of Don Juan Bautista de Anza, Lieutenant Colonel of Cavalry, Governor and Commandant General of the aforesaid province. Showing its towns in their present condition, extremely ill arranged, with the houses of the settlers of whom they are composed scattered about at a distance from one another. Many evils, disaster, and destruction of towns, caused by the Comanche and Apache enemies who surround said province, killing and abducting many families, have originated from this poor arrangement in accordance with which they have taken root, each individual building his dwelling on the piece of land granted to him.[46]

— *Don Bernardo de Miera y Pacheco, 1779*

The pueblos of Christian Indians continue to live according to the same kind of political unity and civilization as when they were heathens and the Spaniards found them when they first came — with their two and three story houses joined together, forming plazas, and all the houses with portable ladders which they pulled up in time of invasion, and the roofs and upper and lower terraces with embrasures in the parapets for their defense and for offense against the enemy.[47]

— *Don Bernardo de Miera y Pacheco, 1779*

The scarcity of seasonal rains experienced in this kingdom for two years past and during the present one has brought such conditions of hunger to the province of Moqui [Hopi], that according to conversations and the frequent news of the month of August last, until today, its dwellers have seen themselves forced to abandon entirely or in greater part their idolatrous pueblos, dividing themselves into many groups among the woods and hills to seek in them wild sustenance. For this reason also they have submitted to various nations whom before they had enriched with what they now lack, their calamities reaching such an extreme that they have sold or are selling their children to procure sustenance.[48]

— *Governor Juan Bautista de Anza, November 1, 1779*

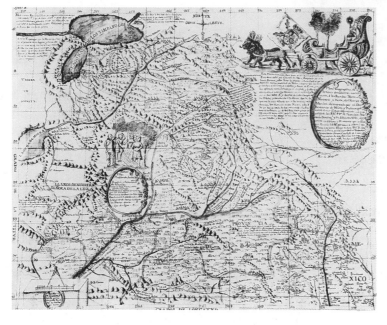

❖ ❖ ❖

Lt. Col. Juan Bautista de Anza, governor of New Mexico (1778–1788), from a painting attributed to Fray Orci in 1774. Original in the Collections of the Palace of the Governors.
(MNM 50828)
The Navajo province of New Mexico in 1778. Map by Don Bernardo de Miera y Pacheco
reflecting the Domínguez-Escalante exploration, in which Miera y Pacheco participated in
1776. Original in the British Library. *(MNM 92063)*

❖ ❖ ❖

Retablo of Santa Rita. Photo by Truman Matthews. *(MNM 21287)*

❖ ❖ ❖

Interior of the Laguna Pueblo mission. The altar dates from ca. 1800.
Photo by T. Harmon Parkhurst, ca. 1935. *(MNM 4870)*

The one named Pedro Vial, who two years ago was commissioned by the governor of Santa Fe to come to these establishments of Illinois, arrived this year as far as the Pawnee nation which has its village on the bank of the Kansas River. There he met our traders [from St. Louis], with whom he remained fifteen days. He said that he came in order that the said Pawnee nation might make peace with the Laytnes [Comanches]. He delivered a medal, a complete suit of clothes, and other things to the chief. He caused peace to be made as he desired, conducting our traders as far as the Comanche nation. In proof of the intentions of the government of both provinces that the said Indians live in friendship, he desires to take our traders to Santa Fe, very near to which vicinity they had [already] arrived, but the latter refused because they did not want to abandon their [own] interests.[49]

— *Zenon Trudeau, commandant at St. Louis, July 4, 1795*

I order you to use great care . . . to prevent the entry into your province by way of neighboring nations of any foreigner or person whatever who may be suspected . . . apprehend those who do come into our territories, if others have accompanied them or if they have been assisted by vassals of the king, gather papers from them.[50]

— *Pedro de Nava, commandant-general of the Interior Provinces, July 30, 1795*

On the eighth of the present month, Josef Miguel Zenguaras, the interpreter in three languages, left with a passport and corresponding instructions and with two Indians from Taos and four *genízaros* [Indian-blooded Spaniards] from the same jurisdiction, to examine the territory that is between this province and the Missouri River. [51]

— *Fernando Chacón, June 10, 1800*

On the fourth of last month, there were presented to me with the interpreter, Don Pedro Vial, whom I commissioned to conduct them from Taos, the two Cuampe [Faraón Apache] chiefs, two Frenchmen from Louisiana, and an American. These latter said they left St. Louis, Illinois, June 8 of this year. . . .

❖ ❖ ❖

Detail of the doors of the old mission church, showing escutcheons of the Dominican and
Franciscan orders. The church is at Santo Domingo Pueblo. Photo by George C. Bennett,
October 1, 1880. *(MNM 14267)*

❖ ❖ ❖

Retablo of Christ entering Jerusalem. *(MNM 48752)*

❖ ❖ ❖

Conquistadora Chapel, built in 1712. In Saint Francis Cathedral in Santa Fe.
Photo by Robert Brewer, 1975. *(MNM 65144)*

❖ ❖ ❖

Nuestra Señora del Rosario, la Conquistadora, in 1930, before restoration by Gustave
Baumann. The statue was brought to New Mexico in 1625.
Photo by T. Harmon Parkhurst. *(MNM 6837)*

. . . Said Frenchmen did not have a passport because, they say, the one their proprietor had when he sent them to trade for beaver, he did not give to them . . . and being poor and without means to return directly to their country, and [being] close to this province, took great pains to show the Cuampes the good treatment of the Spaniards, their good faith and generosity, so much so that they resolved to bring them to Taos. . . .

Those and the American who presented themselves to me destitute, I have assisted meagerly with food and with a minimum of clothing. I resolved to endure this small cost in honor of the good name of the nation, until with their work they can support themselves; but if your Excellency thinks it just to charge this cost to the royal treasury, you will so advise me, and it will turn out that a governor obliged to give alms will not find it necessary to repeat under similar conditions.[52]

— Joaquín de Real Alencaster, governor of New Mexico, July 1, 1805

Its appearance from a distance struck my mind with the same effect as a fleet of the flat bottomed boats which are seen in the spring and fall seasons descending the Ohio River. There are two churches, the magnificance of whose steeples form a striking contrast to the miserable appearance of the houses.[53]

— On the town of Santa Fe, Zebulon M. Pike, March 3, 1807

Here was an old Indian who was extremely inquisitive to know if we were Spaniards, to which an old gentleman called Don Francisco, who appeared to be an intimate of Father Rubi, replied in the affirmative. "But," said the Indian, "they do not speak Castilian." "True," replied the other, "but you are an Indian of the nation of Keres, are you not?" "Yes." "Well, the Utahs are Indians also?" "Yes." "But still you do not understand them, they are speaking a different language." "True," replied the Indian. "Well," said the old gentleman, "those strangers are likewise Spaniards, but [they] do not speak the language with us."[54]

— Zebulon M. Pike, March 6, 1807

❖ ❖ ❖

Corbel from the ruins of the eighteenth-century mission church at Pecos Pueblo. Collections
of the Palace of the Governors. *(HSNM/MNM 14307)*
Copper cross excavated at San Cristóbal Pueblo. Photo by Ernest Johanson, 1955.
(HSNM/MNM 1573)

❖ ❖ ❖

Altar, ca. 1798, in the mission church at Santa Ana Pueblo.
Photo by Odd Halseth, ca. 1923. *(MNM 4072)*

❖ ❖ ❖

Painted wood ornament found in the mission church ruins at Pecos Pueblo. Print from
a damaged negative. Photo by Jesse L. Nusbaum, ca. 1915. (*MNM 41022)*

Both above and below Albuquerque, the citizens were beginning to open the canals to let in the water of the river to fertilize the plains and fields which border its banks on both sides, where we saw men, women, and children of all ages and sexes at joyful labor which was to crown with rich abundance their future harvest and insure them plenty for the ensuing year. Those scenes brought to my recollection the bright descriptions given by Savary of the opening of the canals of Egypt. The cultivation of the fields was now commencing and everything appeared to give life and gaiety to the surrounding scenery.[55]

— *Zebulon M. Pike, March 7, 1807*

Agriculture, industry, and commerce are the three bases of all prosperity. The province of New Mexico has none of these because of its location, because of neglect with which the government has looked upon it up to the present time, and because of the annual withdrawal of the small income that it is able to derive from its products and manufactures . . . the salaries paid by the treasury to the governor of the province, to his assistants, and to the 121 soldiers may be said to be the only income that keeps money in circulation. This income is so small, as we have previously stated, that until recently the majority of its inhabitants had never seen money.[56]

— *Pedro Bautista Pino to the Spanish Cortes, 1812*

The purchase of Louisiana by the United States has opened the way for the Americans to arm and incite the wild Indians against us; also the way is open for the Americans to invade the province. Once this territory is lost, it will be impossible to recover it.[57]

— *Pedro Bautista Pino to the Spanish Cortes, 1812*

None of the provinces in Spanish America can present so good a service record as that of New Mexico. For 118 years that province has maintained a state of warfare with thirty-three wild tribes which surround it, and up to the present time it has not lost one span of land within its old boundaries.[58]

— *Pedro Bautista Pino to the Spanish Cortes, 1812*

❖ ❖ ❖

Early nineteenth-century pine spinning wheel. Photo by Robert Nugent.
Collections of the Palace of the Governors. *(MNM 75798)*

❖ ❖ ❖

Las Trampas, New Mexico, founded in 1760 with the church in the center of town.
Photo by Jesse L. Nusbaum, 1910. *(MNM 36466)*

❖ ❖ ❖

The Severino Martínez house in Taos, ca. 1966. Photo by Keith Green. *(MNM 57315)*

EXPOSICION

SUCINTA Y SENCILLA

DE LA PROVINCIA

DEL

NUEVO MEXICO:

HECHA

POR SU DIPUTADO EN CÓRTES

Don Pedro Baptista Pino,

CON ARREGLO A SUS INSTRUCCIONES.

CÁDIZ:

IMPRENTA DEL ESTADO-MAYOR-GENERAL.

Año de 1812.

❖ ❖ ❖

Lt. Zebulon Pike. From an engraving by Illman Brothers. *(MNM 7757)*
Title page of Pedro Baptista Pino's *Brief Description of New Mexico,* published in Cádiz,
Spain, in 1812. Original in the History Library, Palace of the Governors.
(MNM 152694)

CHAPTER 4

Breaking Away From Spain and Mexico

In 1821 the former Spanish province of New Spain won its independence to become the new Republic of Mexico. Independence had a great effect on its far northern department of New Mexico. A new open-border policy opened up trade with the United States over the Santa Fe Trail. Also, American fur trappers and traders entered the land, bringing with them a foreign culture. The years during which New Mexico was a part of Mexico were chaotic, but the period was short, for with the outbreak of the Mexican War, New Mexico became a part of the United States. It joined as a territory rather than as a state as Congress tried to avoid a civil war.

The President of the Mexican United States to the Republic's inhabitants; know that the general congress has declared that which follows:

All Spaniards who reside in the Western and Eastern internal Territories, the Territories of upper and lower California, and New Mexico, will leave the republic within a month after this law's publication in the state or territory of their residence, and before three months of the law's passage in the republic.[59]

— *Mexican law, March 20, 1829*

❖ ❖ ❖

Brig. Gen. José María Chávez (1801–1902), military officer or civil servant under every governor of New Mexico from Alberto Máynez in 1814 to Miguel Otero in 1897. Photo taken ca. 1895. *(MNM 7116)*
"Looking into a *placita*" in Santa Fe, ca. 1880. Half a stereograph taken by George C. Bennett. *(HSNM/MNM 21043)*

Below lists the number of Spaniards, who through this government have been issued passports for leaving the Republic's territory in conformance and fulfillment of the law of last March 20; and of those that have declared exceptions by another law, with representation of the total number that reside in the Territory of New Mexico.

Fr. Juan Cavallero   Benito Begorchea
Fr. Antonio Cacho   Manuel Alvarez
Fr. Manuel Martínez   Francisco Crain
Manuel Echavarría   Atanasio Bolivar[60]

— Report from New Mexico, 1829

May God grant New Mexico a scientific establishment, where its children may be instructed according to the light of our country![61]

— Santa Fe attorney Antonio Barreiro, 1832

There is an urgent need for more ministers. Almost all the parishes and missions of New Mexico are vacant.[62]

— Antonio Barreiro, 1832

The [New] Mexicans generally are kind, hospitable, intelligent, benevolent and brave. The [New] Mexicans are proud and sensitive people; yet some are more easily subdued by kindness — none more easily won by a ready disposition to mingle in their ranks, and treat them with due respect for their habitude and their prejudices.[63]

— Manuel Alvarez, native of Spain and resident of Santa Fe, 1834

Upon our arrival we found the place full of soldiers, citizens, and a miscellaneous gathering of humanity of all stations of life, the plaza being crowded with all kinds of vehicles, beginning with the cart that was made entirely of wood to the well constructed wagon that had brought a consignment of

❖ ❖ ❖

New Mexican horseman. Watercolor by an unknown artist, possibly Alexander
Barclay in 1853. (Courtesy the Bancroft Library)

❖ ❖ ❖

Altar screen made in 1828, Talpa, New Mexico.
Photo by Shaffer's Studios. *(MNM 48652)*

❖ ❖ ❖

Manuscript copy of an early New Mexican Christmas play, *Los Pastores*. *(MNM 15037)*
Padre Antonio José Martínez, ca. 1848. From a daguerreotype.
(Courtesy Dr. Ward Alan Minge) *(MNM 11262)*

merchandise over the Santa Fe Trail; together with teamsters, camp-cooks, roustabouts, horses, mules, burros, pigs, and goats.[64]

— *On Santa Fe in 1837, Francisco Perea, as remembered in 1914*

There were a great many more dance halls at that time than churches, and they were not wanting in the way of patronage. Every class of building, being constructed of adobe bricks and flat roofed, precluded any great effort at architectural finish.[65]

— *On Santa Fe in 1837, Francisco Perea, as remembered in 1914*

The matter was, these young fellows had grown exhilarated at a *fandango* [dance], and had sallied into the street to whoop and yell and fire off pistols. One of them was expostulating very seriously with a soldier, telling that Santa Fe stood much in need of regulation, and he wished to show him how such things were done in St. Louis.[66]

— *Matthew C. Field, 1840*

It was truly a scene for the artists' pencil to revel in. Even the animals seemed to participate in the humor of their riders, who grew more and more merry and obstreperous as they descended towards the city [Santa Fe]. I doubt, in short, whether the first sight of the walls of Jerusalem were beheld by the crusaders with much more tumultuous and soul enrapturing joy.

The arrival produced a great deal of bustle and excitement among the natives. "*Los Americanos!*" — "*Los carros!*" — "*La entrada de la caravana!*" were to be heard in every direction; and crowds of women and boys flocked around to see the new-comers.[67]

— *Josiah Gregg, 1844*

The Northern Mexicans have often been branded with cowardice: a stigma which may well be allowed to rest upon the wealthier classes. . . . But the rancheros, or as they might be still more appropriately styled — the yeomanry of the country, inured as they are from their peculiar mode of life to every kind of fatigue and danger, possess a much higher calibre of moral courage. . . . I have seen persons of the lower class do things. . . . which would really seem to indicate a superlative degree of courage. Some of them will often perform journeys alone through wildernesses.[68]

— Josiah Gregg, 1844

Notwithstanding their numerous vices, however, I should do the New Mexicans the justice to say that they are but little addicted to inebriety and its attendant dissipations. Yet this doubtlessly results to a considerable degree from the dearness of spirituous liquors, which virtually places them beyond the reach of the lower classes.[69]

— Josiah Gregg, 1844

Yet, notwithstanding this dreadful state of ignorance on all those subjects which it behooves man to be acquainted with, it is truly astonishing to notice the correctness with which common people speak their mother tongue, the Spanish. The application of words out of their classical sense may occasionally occur, but a violation of the simple grammatical rules (which is so common among the illiterate who use the English language), is extremely rare.[70]

— Josiah Gregg, 1844

What a polite people these [New] Mexicans are, altho' they are looked upon as a half barbarous set by the generality of people. This morning I have rather taken a little protégé, a little girl. . . . Just to see the true politeness and ease displayed by that child is truly [amazing], 'twould put many a mother in the U.S. to the blush. And she is so graceful too.[71]

— Susan Shelby Magoffin, September 15, 1846

The women kneeled all over the floor, there being no pews, while men stood up, occasionally kneeling and crossing themselves. The priest neither

❖ ❖ ❖

Teresita Suaso of New Mexico. Watercolor by Alexander Barclay, 1853.
(Courtesy the Bancroft Library)

❖ ❖ ❖

Title page of the original edition of the *Cuaderno de Ortografía,* dedicated to the Martines children of Taos and the first book published in New Mexico (in Santa Fe, 1834) *(MNM 45009)* General Manuel Armijo, Mexican governor of New Mexico (1827–1829, 1837–1844, 1845–1846). From a drawing, ca. 1845. Original in the Palace of the Governors. *(MNM 50809)*

❖ ❖ ❖

Spanish or Mexican *carreta* of cottonwood and willow, Tesuque Pueblo.
Photo by Dana B. Chase, ca. 1890. (*MNM 11827*)

preached nor prayed, leaving each one to pray for himself; he repeated some Latin neither understood by himself or his hearers. The latter repeated their *aves* and *pater nosters*. . . . Their music consisted of a violin, which all of the time they continued to tune, and a thumming gingling guitar; the same tunes they had the other night at the *fandango,* were played.[72]

— *Susan Shelby Magoffin, September 20, 1846*

This is the first day I have dined at table for two whole weeks. I found my way out as dinner came in, and sat down to table. Our dinner of chili with *carne de carnero* [mutton], stewed chicken with *cibollas* [cebollas or onions], and a dessert made of bread and grapes, a kind of pudding I suppose, was furnished by our lord and lady.

Tonight the Priestly portion of the community followed by a crowd, has paraded the patron St. of San Gabriel, with the cross bourn before it, around the *plazo* [plaza], which was illuminated by many small heaps of burning wood and tourches bourn by the procession . . . the music I believe consisted of a kind of drum, violins and I suppose the ever constant accompaniment of the triangle. . . .

It is rather odd to see the women coming from other towns in ox-carts, alias, Rio Baja steamboats. The whole family, wife, children, servants, dogs and all get, or rather pile themselves, up in the vehicle of all work and the *dueno de todos* [their lord and master], with his long pole gets his horned animals under way, and off they start squeaking, squeaking, barking and other noises accompanying such crowds.[73]

— *Susan Shelby Magoffin, San Gabriel, New Mexico, November 18, 1846*

I learned last night their [New Mexicans'] mode of giving a sweat. The patient is made to sit with his feet in warm water, in which has been boiled some wheat-brand, with blankets thrown over him till a profuse perspiration is produced, assisted by drinking some warm tea or hot lemonade. After persevering in this some fifteen minutes, he is covered up in bed, some dirt is now put into a plate, a little fire on this; a few pounded annice seed and black

❖ ❖ ❖

Dr. Josiah Gregg, trader over the Santa Fe Trail, ca. 1845. *(MNM 9896)*
James P. Beckwourth, trapper, trader, and mountain man. From *Harper's New Monthly Magazine,* September 1856. *(MNM 8798)*

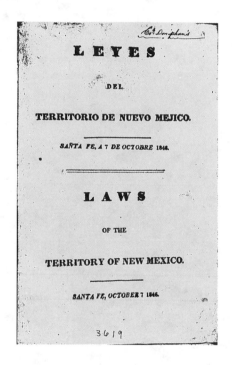

Albuquerque house interior. From a watercolor sketch of the residence of Padre José Manuel Gallegos. Reprinted in John Galvin, ed., *Western America in 1846: The Original Travel Diary of Lieutenant J. W. Abert* (San Francisco, 1966). *(MNM 113651)*
Title page of the original edition of the *Laws of the Territory of New Mexico,* published in Santa Fe in 1846. Also known as the Kearny Code, these were the first official laws under the United States administration in New Mexico. Copy in History Library, Palace of the Governors. *(MNM 47335)*

❖ ❖ ❖

Hos-ta (The Lightning), governor of Jémez Pueblo. From a watercolor by Richard H. Kern,
August 20, 1849. From Senate Ex. Doc. 1st Session, 31st Congress, No. 64. *(MNM 14854)*

❖ ❖ ❖

Jémez Pueblo by Richard H. Kern.
Senate Ex. Doc. 1st Session, 31st Congress, No. 64. *(MNM 2796)*

peppers are then thrown onto it, and it is set under the bed cloths till the invalid, bed and all, become perfectly hot from it. It is both a simple and good method.[74]

— Susan Shelby Magoffin, December 15, 1846

When the concluding words *"muerto, muerto, muerto"* — dead, dead, dead — were pronounced by Judge Beaubien in his solemn and impressive manner, the painful stillness that reigned in the courtroom and the subdued grief manifested by a few bystanders were noticed not without an inward sympathy. The poor wretches sat with immovable features; but I fancied that under the assumed looks of apathetic indifference could be read the deepest anguish. When remanded to jail till the day of execution, they drew their *serapes* more closely around them and accompanied the armed guard. I left the room, sick at heart. Justice! Out upon the word, when its distorted meaning is the warrant for murdering those who defend to the last their country and their homes.[75]

— On the Taos trials of accused revolutionaries against American occupation,
Lewis H. Garrard, 1847

Having embraced Christianity under the Spanish rule, the Pueblos were admitted to the rights of citizenship by the Mexican government under Iturbide, and these rights which they have enjoyed to the present time (at least in name) are confirmed to them by the state constitution. Under this they are subject to taxation (by legislation) in common with the other inhabitants. It is to be hoped, however, the legislature will, in its wisdom, adopt a mild and conciliatory policy toward these people. Under the present change of government . . . dissatisfaction produced at the outset may ultimately lead to more serious results than would at first glance appear. To explain this it will be necessary to state in what way the Pueblos may be made an element of much good or evil to the state.[76]

— U.S. Army Col. George Archibald McCall, July 1850

The lower class are as ignorant as idle, and even among their superiors education is woefully neglected.

❖ ❖ ❖

William S. Messervy, ca. 1849, trader over the Santa Fe Trail and acting governor of New
Mexico in 1853. From a daguerreotype. *(MNM 88121)*
Charles H. Trotier, Sieur de Beaubien, judge (1846–1851) and merchant, ca. 1850. Copy
photo by Nicholas and Howard after a daguerreotype. *(MNM 8799)*

❖ ❖ ❖

Blacksmith shop in Zuni Pueblo. From a drawing by Richard H. Kern, as lithographed
by James Ackerman for the report of the U.S. government's
Sitgreaves expedition, 1853. *(MNM 38177)*

From this it may be inferred that no great improvement in the moral condition of the present generation can be expected from the introduction of our institutions, which they can neither understand nor appreciate. It is to the coming generation we must look for this; and, therefore, the introduction of primary schools, at as early a day as practicable, is a consideration of much interest.[77]

— *U.S. Army Col. George Archibald McCall, July 1850*

In September last six boys and two women [Navajos] left their camp with some *piñones* to sell, at Cubera — close to Laguna, they sold some of the *piñones,* and on the same day returned towards their homes, night overtook them and they camped about two leagues from Pueblo Santa Ana, Juan Gonzales a Mexican, the *alcalde* of the town of Cubera at present, left the Pueblo of Santa Ana, with eight or ten Indians of the pueblo and fell upon the party, and captured six animals after the robbing party took the animals. The Navajos ran away for they were scared, but instead of running the way from danger, they ran upon the *alcalde* who had taken their animals. The Pueblo Indians ran off, and left the *alcalde,* then the Navajos took from the *alcalde* a mare, saddle, bridle, and rifle all the property of the *alcalde*. The Navajos are willing to let the *alcalde* keep three of their animals, one for the mare, one for the saddle and bridle and one for the rifle.[78]

— *Indian agent John Greiner, April 13, 1852*

The Comanches have not been in this vicinity and we hear of them but little, except that they are now gathering upon the Arkansas for the purpose of trading, hunting buffalo, and as is their usual practice in the spring.

A Pueblo Indian who had been trading with them, and who speaks their language fluently, states, that one of their principal chiefs had just returned from the City of Mexico, and appeared to be very solicitous of forming a league with the other wild tribes of Texas and New Mexico for the alleged purpose of uniting with the Mexicans to expel or exterminate the Americans now in this country.[79]

— *John Greiner, April 30, 1852*

One of the band of Capote Eutaws [Ute Indians] was taken sick not long ago, and a doctor belonging to the Sieveritch Eutaws was called in to attend him. In a few days the patient died.

A meeting of the Capotes was called and the doctor was tried. His sentence was to be shot and scalped, his wife's hair to be cut off, his animals killed, and his house burned, all of which was instantly carried into effect.[80]

— John Greiner, April 30, 1852

Heard that Jicarillas had killed six sheep in the Bosque Redondo and killed all the dogs belonging to the *pastores;* sheep belonged to Manuel Chavez.[81]

— John Greiner, May 21, 1852

Ordered by Richard Campbell, Probate Judge in and for the County of Doña Ana and Territory of New Mexico, that the holes made in the Streets of the Town of Las Cruces for the purpose of making adobes and for other purposes be filled up within thirty days from the issuing of this order with the positive assurance that all those who made such holes and do not fill them up or comply with this order within thirty days from the date hereof will be fined and legal steps taken to compel the payment of such fines.[82]

— By order of Richard Campbell, Probate Judge, September 17, 1853

After the organization of the volunteers, the Governor appointed Captain Ceran St. Vrain of Taos, as their Commander. He was a gentleman in every manner qualified for such office, the greater part of his life having been passed in the mountains and this Territory.

And when the people became aware of the Governor having chosen a man so competent to fulfill the duties of an office of such importance there was great rejoicing, for all knew the Captain to be a gentleman and the bravest of soldiers. And now were confident that, under the command of such a man that the Indians would be punished in such a manner that it would be long before they would again commence hostilities. In fact, it was the only appointment of

❖ ❖ ❖

William Workman, merchant and trader, ca. 1855. From a daguerreotype. *(MNM 13492)*
Brig. Gen. Henry H. Sibley, commander of the Confederate Army of invasion of
New Mexico, ca. 1862. *(MNM 50541)*

the Governor that met the approbation of the people. Many were surprised at his sound judgement making such a noble choice.[83]

— *Christopher (Kit) Carson, trader, trapper, and colonel in the U.S. Army, 1854*

I cannot know how the Superintendent can expect Indians to depart satisfied [that] he has called [them] to see him from a distance of two or three hundred miles, compelled [them] to go several days without anything to eat, unless they have carried it with them.

They are given a meal by the Superintendent, then the presents are given. Some get a blanket; those that get none, are given a knife or hatchet or some vermillion, a piece of red or blue cloth, some sugar and perhaps a few more trinkets. They could more than earn the quantity they receive in one day's hunt if left in their own country. They could procure skins and furs and traders could furnish the same articles to them and they would be saved the necessity of coming such a distance, thereby not causing their animals to be fatigued and themselves have to travel without food. . . .

. . . for every visit an Indian makes to a town, it is of more or less injury to him.[84]

— *Christopher (Kit) Carson, 1858*

The smallpox is prevailing at all points in the Mesilla Valley though generally in a mild form. It is prevailing among the Confederate soldiers, one company having twelve cases up to date. Two have died. The sick are provided with comfortable quarters and receive every care and attention.[85]

— The Mesilla Times, *December 19, 1861*

GENERAL: I have the honor to herewith enclose the report of Major David Fergusson, 1st [C]avalry California volunteers, whom I ordered to make a survey of [P]ort Lobos and Libertad, on the [G]ulf of California. This is a report of great importance, as showing how much cheaper supplies can be gotten for Arizona and the Mesilla [V]alley, via Libertad, than from Indianola, Texas, or from Kansas City. The report is of still greater importance when

❖ ❖ ❖

"The Centenarians," Juan Jesús Rivera (age 106) in Santa Fe, ca. 1880.
Half a stereograph by George C. Bennett. *(MNM 15348)*

considered with reference to the political and commercial geography of our country. It shows how very important it is for us to purchase from Mexico, before it becomes a possession of, say, France, a strip of territory which will give us so fine and accessible a port on the [G]ulf of California.

When the vast mineral resources of Arizona and of the Pinos Altos region have become better known (and not one year will pass away before this importance will be appreciated), then the government will see that a port on the [G]ulf of California should be ours, at any cost.[86]

— Brig. Gen. James H. Carleton to Brig. Gen. Lorenzo Thomas,
Adj. Gen., U.S. Army, February 1, 1863

❖ ❖ ❖

Tom Toslino (Navajo) as he arrived at the Training School, Carlisle, Pennsylvania, ca. 1880.
Photo by John N. Choate. *(MNM 43501)*

❖ ❖ ❖

Tom Toslino (Navajo) after three years at the Training School, Carlisle, Pennsylvania, ca. 1883. Photo by John N. Choate. *(MNM 43500)*

CHAPTER 5

Territorial New Mexico After the Civil War

After almost two and a half centuries under the rule of Madrid and Mexico City, New Mexico was suddenly a part of the young United States, a country that had recently and violently established itself. After the Civil War, New Mexico entered into a new modern era, at once wondrous and awful, accompanied by indifferent governments, the railroad, range wars, the Rough Riders, and new lifestyles. Mexican Hispanics, Indians, and newly arrived people from the East had to learn to live together — and some preferred not to coexist. Everyone had to learn to live in a new modern world that was engulfing them.

From the time of the Gadsden purchase, when we came into possession of their country, until about ten years ago, the Apaches were the friends of the Americans. Much of the time since then, the attempt to exterminate them has been carried on, at a cost of from three to four millions of dollars per annum, with no appreciable progress being made in accomplishing their extermination.[87]

— *Board of Indian Commissioners, Washington, D.C., December 12, 1871*

Mr. Editor — I am a poor carpenter, but do not steal my trade from Uncle Sam. Somebody said that two foot of snow will break down the roof of Mrs.

❖ ❖ ❖

José Quivera, the governor of San Felipe Pueblo, using a twist drill.
Photo by John K. Hillers, 1880. *(MNM 3415)*

Manuela Chaves' building; he can get on top of it with all his money, and I will be responsible for the roof. Another says the first wind that comes will blow it over; I say that he can devour *dos fanegas de frijol* and blow all his poisen with the wind and I will still be responsible for the roof.[88]

— *George Fournier,* The Santa Fe Daily New Mexican, *June 24, 1873*

Everything in New Mexico that pays at all (you may say) is worked by a "ring." There is the "Indian ring," the "army ring," and "legal ring," the "Roman ring," the "cattle ring," the "horse thieves ring," the "land ring," and half a dozen other rings. Now "to make things stick" to do any good it is necessary to either get into a ring or make one for yourself. I am work[ing] at present making a ring.[89]

— *John Henry Tunstall to his father, April 27, 1877*

The United States ought to declare war on Mexico and make it take back New Mexico.[90]

— *Gen. William T. Sherman to Territorial Governor Lew Wallace, 1878*

New Mexico has hitherto been little known in the east, but this is now changed. With easy rapid communication assured, her wonderful advantages can now be heralded to the world with a certainty that attention will be attracted. Invalids will come to recuperate, and build up exhausted constitutions, capitalists will be drawn here by the great mineral wealth of the Territory, and the pleasure seeker and tourist will come to revel in the delights of our mountain scenery.[91]

— The Santa Fe New Mexican, *February 27, 1880*

You [New Mexicans] must improve your land and develop the vast resources of your country, or the new race will come in here and displace you. I hope and pray that the next time I come here I shall surely find the old race of Mexicans that we found here long, long ago in the past, improved — brought

❖ ❖ ❖

A New Mexican ranch. From Horatio O. Ladd, *The Story of New Mexico* (Boston, 1891).
(MNM 152693)
Juan María de Agostini, the hermit of Hermit's Peak, near Las Vegas, New Mexico,
before 1864. *(MNM 110777)*

❖ ❖ ❖

Gen. Ulysses S. Grant and family, Santa Fe, July 14, 1880. Half a stereograph by Ben Wittick. *(MNM 39392)*

Masonic group, Santa Fe, December 26, 1866. Standing left to right: Lt. Col. Edward H. Bergman, congressional delegate Charles P. Clever, Col. Nelson H. Davis, Col. Herbert M. Enos (Quartermaster General of New Mexico Military District), Surgeon Basil K. Norris, Col. J. C. McFerran. Seated left to right: Col. D. H. Rucker, Bvt. Brig. Gen. Christopher "Kit" Carson, Bvt. Gen. James H. Carleton. *(MNM 9826)*

❖ ❖ ❖

New Mexico Militia officers, 1883. Left to right: Capt. Eugene Van Patten, Lt. Pedro
Pedragon, Maj. Albert Fountain, 2nd Lt. Albert Fountain, Jr., Capt. Francisco
Salazar, Lt. Maclovio Botello. (*HSNM/MNM 13148*)
Maj. Gen. Lew Wallace, Civil War general, author of *Ben Hur,* governor of New Mexico
(1878–1881). Photo ca. 1862–1865 (detail). (*MNM 77788*)

to a higher degree of improvement and cultivation. Without that they will be displaced, not by force, injustice and violence, but by a better, stronger higher race, that will develop the resources of the country. New Mexico has a pretty hard name all over the world; I have said some pretty hard things of New Mexico; I have no feeling against the people. The people sit here and growl and eat garlic.

You must . . . get rid of your burros and goats: I hope ten years hence there won't be an adobe house in the Territory. I want to see you learn to make them of brick, with slanting roofs. Yankees don't like flat roofs, nor roofs of dirt.[92]

— *Address of Gen. William T. Sherman in Santa Fe, October 28, 1880*

Every calculation based on experience elsewhere, fails in New Mexico.[93]

— *Territorial Governor Lew Wallace, 1878–1881*

From the year 1880 dates the advent of the railroad into the Rio Grande — from thence communicating through the cardinal points of the world. Manifestly, it is an event to be fraught with the grandest results ever yet known to this most ancient and historical land.[94]

— *Territorial Secretary William G. Ritch, February 21, 1881*

The citizens of this city [Socorro] were surprised in finding the stiffs of Clark and Frenchy . . . hanging chained together in a narrow street just off the plaza called "death's alley," with a placard on their backs saying: "This is the way Socorro treats horse thieves, and footpads."[95]

— *On Socorro,* The Santa Fe New Mexican, *October 8, 1881*

Not all Americans are as bad as the authorities: found many with very equitable feeling towards the Mexicans, and who strongly disclaim any connection with the offensive conduct of some big men here.[96]

— *Adolph F. Bandelier, November 2, 1881*

❖ ❖ ❖

Acequia Madre in Albuquerque, ca. 1881–1884.
Photo by Ben Wittick. *(SAR/MNM 15754)*

126

❖ ❖ ❖

Fireplace of an old Spanish house in Taos, 1881. Photo by
William Henry Jackson. *(MNM 51943)*

❖ ❖ ❖

Navajo silversmith. *(MNM 91455)*

❖ ❖ ❖

Street in Old Town, Albuquerque, ca. 1881. Photo by Ben Wittick.
(SAR/MNM 15753)

❖ ❖ ❖

Henry Clay gold mine, White Oaks, New Mexico.
(Johnson Stearns Papers, RGHC MS 98)

❖ ❖ ❖

Las Vegas College (Jesuit), opened in 1877 in a house belonging to Francisco López.
Photo by James H. Furlong, ca. 1878. *(MNM 66005)*
Archbishop Jean Baptiste Lamy, ca. 1880–1882. Copy photo by William Henry Brown.
(HSNM/MNM 9970)

❖ ❖ ❖

Former Zuni Pueblo governor, Palowatiwa Nanahe (a Hopi married into Zuni),
and former Pueblo governor Pedro Pino, Zuni Pueblo.
Photo by John K. Hillers, 1879–1880. *(MNM 73898)*

❖ ❖ ❖

Capt. Jack Crawford, the "Poet Scout," ca. 1881–1884.
Photo by Ben Wittick. *(MNM 102037)*

❖ ❖ ❖

Juan José Montoya and his daughter Ignacia in an arrangement of artifacts
for Adolph F. Bandelier at Cochiti Pueblo on November 30, 1880.
Photo by George C. Bennett. *(MNM 2490)*

134

Luckily someone was found to tune the piano. Musicals followed, attended by whoever might come — and there were plenty. Those young men were mostly miners and apparently roughnecks, yet a surprising number were college graduates and from cultured families. And how they loved to sing! Mother sent for half a dozen or more gospel hymn books and an equal number of collections of college songs. The boys sent for some special things themselves. Soon other instruments appeared: a violin, a flute, a guitar, a banjo. But the piano was always in the lead. Other activities developed with the singing. We had recitations, readings, talks, even a "Literary Club," at that time the rage.[97]

— On White Oaks in 1880–1882, Morris B. Parker, as written in 1948

These were the embryonic days of White Oaks, and they were no doubt full of fun, tragedy, and disappointment — local history in the making. Between the ages of eleven and fourteen, however, I was too young to be greatly impressed by such matters. Nevertheless the mixed character and culture of the residences, both mobile and fixed, was evident. They ranged from ignorant nomads — cowboys and prospectors — to college graduates. They included good men and bad, gold-hungry adventurers and people who just came to look around. Horace Greeley's widely publicized advice — "Go West, young man, go West!" — was the motivating force for the latter group.[98]

— On White Oaks in 1880–1882, Morris B. Parker, as written in 1948

No member shall be held responsible elsewhere for words spoken in debate or for his vote.[99]

— Rules of the Legislative Assembly, Twenty-fifth Session, 1882

Civic societies are represented in Masonry, Odd Fellowship, Good Templars and Knights of Pythias. The Historical Society has been revived at Santa Fe. Gas light, water-works, the telephone, horse and railroads are among the modern improvements found at Santa Fe, Las Vegas, and Albuquerque.

❖ ❖ ❖

Susan McSween Barber, a survivor of the Lincoln County Wars, in which her husband was
shot to death. *(Courtesy Special Collections, University of Arizona Library)*
Frank Hamilton Cushing in a costume of his own design as a Zuni Pueblo Priest of the Bow,
March 1882. Photo probably by James Wallace Black. *(MNM 9147)*

❖ ❖ ❖

Man with pistol in Hillsboro or Kingston, New Mexico, ca. 1885–1892.
Photo by J. C. Burge. *(BRM/MNM 76778)*
Jesús Silva and Richens Lacy "Uncle Dick" Wootton, trapper, trader, freighter, merchant,
frontiersman, in 1885. Photo by Harold Elderkin. *(MNM 13112)*

❖ ❖ ❖

Tennis at Kingston, ca. 1885–1892.
Photo by J. C. Burge. *(John L. Gregg Collection, RCHC RG80-14)*

❖ ❖ ❖

False stone figures made by a Pueblo Indian for sale to tourists, ca. 1895–1900.
(MNM 781)

Work train with locomotive number 85 (Baldwin, 1879) in Engle, New Mexico, ca. 1890.
Photo by E. J. Westervelt. *(MNM 35876)*

❖ ❖ ❖

Agneda Salazar in wedding dress, Las Vegas, New Mexico, ca. 1890–1891.
Photo probably by Theron Crispell. *(MNM 7637)*

❖ ❖ ❖

"Coming of the Gramophone," Baldy, New Mexico, ca. 1891.
Photo by William A. White. *(MNM 14636)*

In nothing, save in the rapid building of railroads, is there better evidence of substantial progress than in the development of the press of the territory.[100]

— William G. Ritch, 1882

Silver City, the metropolis of the southwest, also has a railroad projected for connection with the continental system at Deming.[101]

— William G. Ritch, 1882

The [1883] Tertio-Millennial parade in Santa Fe, held in celebration of the third century of the coming of the Spaniards to settle in New Mexico, was a great success. I was not able to take an active part because I was in jail for contempt of court, at the time, but the sheriff was kind enough to allow his prisoners to view the parade from the streets.[102]

— Miguel Antonio Otero, 1939

Many years ago a few sharp shrewd Americans came here — discovered a number of small Mexican and Spanish [Land] Grants — purchased them at nominal prices — learned the Spanish language — ingratiated themselves into favor with the Mexican people, and proceeded to enlarge the Grants they had purchased, and to manufacture at will, titles to still others, and to secure therefore Congressional recognition.[103]

— Governor Edmund G. Ross, March 26, 1887

New Mexico, like the dearest of women, cannot be adequately photographed. One can reproduce the features, but not the expression — the landmarks, but not the wondrous light which is to the bare Southwest the soul that glorifies the plain face.[104]

— Charles Lummis, 1893

❖ ❖ ❖

Francis Schlatter, faith healer, in 1892. Photo by William A. White.
(From a damaged original print.) *(MNM 91346)*
Daughters of William Manderfield and Josefa Salazar, ca. 1893–1895. Left to right: Cyrilla,
Josefita (front), Eugénia, Florentina. *(HSNM/MNM 10287)*

144

❖ ❖ ❖

Cattle pen, Deming, New Mexico, ca. 1890–1895. *(MNM 12706)*

❖ ❖ ❖

Scene in Zuni Pueblo, ca. 1891–1896.
Photo by Matilda Coxe Stevenson. *(MNM 82373)*

146

❖ ❖ ❖

After a sandstorm, Deming, New Mexico, April 13, 1895. *(MNM 12156)*

❖ ❖ ❖

Santa Fe County sheriff Milo Martínez and his wife, Las Vegas, ca. 1895.
Photo by James N. Furlong. *(MNM 12114)*
A Spanish family in Mora Valley, New Mexico, September 1895. *(MNM 22467)*

❖ ❖ ❖

Funeral procession in Mora, New Mexico, 1895.
Photo by Tom Walton. *(MNM 14757)*

149

❖ ❖ ❖

Navajo weavers with Arbuckle's coffee box, ca. 1895. *(MNM 808)*

❖ ❖ ❖

Col. Theodore Roosevelt at the first Rough Riders Reunion at the Castañeda Hotel
in Las Vegas, June 1899. *(MNM 14292)*

❖ ❖ ❖

Baking in an *horno* in Santa Fe, ca. 1898–1900. Photo by Christian G. Kaadt.
(MNM 69106)

❖ ❖ ❖

Procession of La Conquistadora on San Francisco Street in Santa Fe, June 1897.
Photo by Philip Embury Harroun. *(MNM 8120)*
Mud plastering an adobe wall in Abiquiu, New Mexico, ca. 1897.
Photo by Philip Embury Harroun. *(MNM 12535)*

❖ ❖ ❖

Railroad section gang in Cubrero, New Mexico, ca. 1900.
Photo by Emil Bibo. *(MNM 44817)*

❖ ❖ ❖

Burro packing wagon wheels at the Harvey Ranch at Elk Mountain
(near Las Vegas), ca. 1900. *(MNM 15181)*

❖ ❖ ❖

A dam at North Spring River near Roswell, New Mexico, ca. 1900. *(MNM 57868)*

Society is little bitten with the unrest of civilization. The old ways are still the best ways; and the increasing reprobates who would improve upon their fathers are eyed askance. The social system is patriarchal, and in many degrees beautiful. Mexican and Pueblo children are, as a class, the best-mannered, the most obedient, the least quarrelsome in America. Respect for age is the cornerstone of society. A son, untouched by our refining influence, would as soon put his hand in the fire as smoke before his parents — even though he has already given them grand-children. A stranger, be he poor or princely, is master of the house to which he shall come.[105]

— *Charles Lummis, 1893*

As the midnight wind sweeps that weird strain down the lonely canyon, it seems the wail of a lost spirit. I have known men of tried bravery to flee from that sound when they heard it for the first time. A simple air on a fife made of the *cariso* seems a mild matter to read of; but its wild shriek, which can be heard for miles, carries an indescribable terror with it.[106]

— *Charles Lummis, 1893*

[T]he invariable defensive sites are eloquent witnesses to the dangers of old, when every first thought must be for safety from the crowding savage. Convenience, even to water, was a secondary consideration. Of this, Acoma is the most striking type. No other town on earth is so nobly perched. The only foreign hints of it are the Konigstein, in Saxony; and (perhaps) the Gwalior, in the Deccan.[107]

— *Charles Lummis, 1893*

But a few rods north of the [Abó] pueblo tower the giant walls of a noble edifice — such walls as would have been long ago immortalized in American literature, were they in Rhinish Bavaria instead of a land which might be fancied to have a patriotic interest to Americans. Amid the talus of tumbled stone these two vast walls, forty-two feet apart, one hundred and fifteen feet long and twelve feet thick at the base, soar sixty feet aloft in rugged majesty.

❖ ❖ ❖

"Tough Hombres of Wagon Mound," ca. 1900. Fabian Chávez, the author's grandfather,
at the right. Nora Chávez Collection. *(MNM 113653)*

❖ ❖ ❖

Postcard with note, Bullard Street, Silver City, New Mexico, ca. 1900.
(Amador Family Papers, RGHC MS 4)
Family group in Mayhill, New Mexico, ca. 1900–1915. Photo by Green Edward Miller.
(MNM 102782)

❖ ❖ ❖

County law officers, Church Street, Las Cruces, New Mexico. Left to right: Felipe Lucero,
Bob Birch, Morgan Llewellyn. *(RGHC A76-157/128)*

❖ ❖ ❖

Mayhill, New Mexico, February 9, 1904. Photo by Green Edward Miller. *(RGHC MS 101)*

❖ ❖ ❖

Hauling broom corn in Clovis, New Mexico, ca. 1905. *(MNM 8987)*

162

❖ ❖ ❖

Firing pottery at Santa Clara Pueblo, 1904–1905.
Photo by Edward S. Curtis. *(MNM 31940)*

❖ ❖ ❖

Husking corn in northern New Mexico, ca. 1905.
Photo by Edwin S. Andrews. *(MNM 71218)*

❖ ❖ ❖

M. R. Martínez and family, Chimayó, New Mexico, ca. 1905. *(MNM 21035)*

165

❖ ❖ ❖

"Uncle" Tom Barkley, probably at Mayhill, New Mexico, ca. 1905. Barkley's legs froze in a
blizzard while he was herding sheep in the Sacramento Mountains. After an amputation
he refused to wear artificial legs and walked on his knees. Here he holds a Bible open
to the Book of Acts. Photo by Green Edward Miller. *(MNM 102771)*

❖ ❖ ❖

"The Wolf" (Navajo), ca. 1906. Photo by Carl Moon. *(MNM 70413)*

❖ ❖ ❖

The "Mountain Pride" stagecoach at G. T. Miller Drug Store in Hillsboro, New Mexico, ca. 1905–1908. Photo by George T. Miller. *(MNM 76905)*

Their ancient masonry of darkly-rufous sandstone, in adobe mortar, is almost perfect in alignment still.[108]

— *On Abó, Charles Lummis, 1893*

It was in 1900 soon after I'd been elected sheriff for the first time. Pat Garrett held office from 1895 until 1900 when he decided not to run again. I was a young man to hold such a position for those were tough times in New Mexico and Doña Ana [C]ounty had a record of crime.

But I won the election and no sooner had I taken office than hell started popping. The first murder took place on New Year's eve, didn't even give me time to get into harness. A man was killed in the Tip-Top saloon in Cruces. When I got to the office on New Year's I found Pat, evidently thinking I was too inexperienced to be trusted with a murder case on the first day, had sent the murderer, under the care of the jailer, to El Paso authorities.

By the time I'd been in office three days and had got my boots under the desk there was a second murder, this time at Mesilla. I spent the rest of my first week trailing man and dog tracks through the bosques, for the murderer's little dog followed him in his flight and we finally picked them up as they were drinking at the river.

When the third murder came along within a couple of weeks I was an old, experienced officer. It occurred near the site of the recent train robbery and murder which they're making such a to-do about today, on the Southern Pacific railroad near Lanark. A passenger was watching the jack rabbits and the cactus roll by when he caught sight of smoke pouring out of a culvert. They stopped the train and found the body of a boy, shot in the back at such close range that his clothing had caught on fire.

At the next station four suspicious looking men boarded the train and the conductor held them for El Paso authorities. They called me to question the suspects and I let two of them go but brought back to jail with me an old Mexico Indian, Toribio Huerta, and a boy who said he came from Albuquerque. Huerta was the murderer right enough. I got the story out of the boy, and then Huerta confessed. . . . Huerta had killed him for $45 and forced the other boy to help stuff the body under the culvert.

❖ ❖ ❖

Burro in a street at Acoma Pueblo, 1908. Photo by H. F. Robinson. *(MNM 36675)*

❖ ❖ ❖

Musicians near Mayhill, ca. 1910. Photo by Green Edward Miller. *(RGHC RG81-6-5)*

❖ ❖ ❖

Tourists at Santo Domingo Pueblo, ca. 1910. *(MNM 4337)*

❖ ❖ ❖

Taos Pueblo painter, ca. 1910–1915. Photo by George L. Beam. *(MNM 86249)*

173

❖ ❖ ❖

Ralph Emerson Twitchell, New Mexico historian, ca. 1910. *(MNM 7902)*
Load of hay from W. E. Baker Ranch, Las Cruces, 1911. *(RGHC A76-157/45)*

Huerta was due for a hanging and I was the man to do it. No, I didn't mind. He was a murderer and had to pay the penalty. I was the sheriff and had to do my duty. . . .

"Sheriff, don't spring me too quick!" Huerta begged. So we let him make a speech to his audience and he advised the young men who'd come to watch him die, not to set their feet on the path of crime. Then we tied the black cap over his head, but still he wasn't ready. We let him pray there in the darkness. Finally I said, "Ready Huerta?" and he nodded — for weeks it was a byword around town, "Ready Huerta?" Soon a law was passed prohibiting public executions.[109]

— On the last public hanging in Las Cruces, 1900, as told by José Lucero to Margaret Page Hood, The New Mexico Sentinel, *January 26, 1938*

❖ ❖ ❖

Mother and child at Jémez Pueblo, ca. 1910–1912.
Photo by Jesse L. Nusbaum. *(MNM 61712)*

❖ ❖ ❖

LeBaron Bradford Prince, chief justice of New Mexico (1879–1882), governor of New
Mexico (1889–1893), president of the Historical Society of New Mexico.
Photo ca. 1910. *(MNM 50444)*
Solomon Luna, sheep rancher, banker, politician, and *patron* of the Luna Land Grant.
(MNM 50606)

177

❖ ❖ ❖

Bridge near Maxwell, New Mexico, ca. 1912. *(MNM 848)*

CHAPTER 6

Eventually a New State

More than three centuries after its first European settlement, New Mexico became the forty-seventh state of the Union. Now an equal in its adoptive country, it harbored old and new traditions that had to coexist. Over time, both lifestyles persisted. Within miles of one another, centuries-old villages existed with modern, secret laboratories developing atomic power and laser technology. Today, the people still struggle to maintain a cultural identity while learning to be full participants in a modern society.

The constitution formulated by the convention which closes today contains 20,000 words, 130 sections grouped into twenty-two articles. Probably no other commonwealth ever was confronted by the peculiar difficulties that faced the constitutional convention when it convened. Unique and paramount, despite repeated denial, was the race and language question.[110]

— The Santa Fe New Mexican, *November 21, 1910*

All New Mexico today rejoices over the signing of the statehood bill by President Taft.

In fact the joy making has not been of today only but has been really "triduum" in variety, for it began in Santa Fe Saturday afternoon when the *New*

❖ ❖ ❖

New Mexico Constitutional Convention in Santa Fe, 1910.
Photo by William R. Walton. *(MNM 8119)*

Mexican announced the news flashed from Washington that the House had concurred in the Senate bill. This city witnessed a demonstration of the people's joy Saturday night when a mass meeting was held in the plaza and presided over by Acting Governor Nathan Jaffa. . . .[111]

— The Santa Fe New Mexican, *June 20, 1912*

All I remember about the people living there was the huge refugee camp. Decent hard working families had come across the border to find a place where banditry was now under control. They lived in wagons and make-shift tents. I was impressed with the efforts of these displaced people to keep clean. The mothers did not forget to bring along their wash tubs. Clothes lines with freshly cleaned garments hung in the sun. . . . As I walked around town I passed some skeletons of horses killed in the Villa raid. The chalky white bones, cleaned by carniverous animals and insects, were just across the line on the Mexican side — a symbolic reminder that had brought a vast American Army to the border.[112]

— *On Columbus, New Mexico, after Pancho Villa's raid,*
journalist Harold Palmer Brown, 1916

To what composite American identity of the future, Spanish character will supply some of the most needed part. No stock shows a grander historic retrospect — grander in religiousness and loyalty, or for patriotism, courage, decorum, gravity and honor.[113]

— *Walt Whitman,* The Santa Fe New Mexican, *September 7, 1918*

I ain't goin' to quit saying ain't.[114]

— *Albuquerque Commission Chairman Clyde Tingly,*
The Albuquerque Journal, *June 16, 1926,*

❖ ❖ ❖

Winter view of Mogollon, 1914. A calendar photograph. *(RGHC A76-40)*
Building a concrete silo on C. H. Smith Farm, Mesilla Valley, 1917. *(RGHC RG78-82/5)*

❖ ❖ ❖

Man feeding chickens in Santa Fe, ca. 1915–1920. Photo probably by Wesley Bradfield.
(MNM 47757)

❖ ❖ ❖

Group of children, possibly in Santa Fe, ca. 1915. Photo by Kenneth Chapman.
(MNM 27986)

❖ ❖ ❖

Spanish wedding group in Santa Fe, 1912. Photo by Jesse L. Nusbaum. *(MNM 61817)*

❖ ❖ ❖

Wedding portrait in Santa Fe, 1912. Photo by Jesse L. Nusbaum. *(MNM 61804)*

❖ ❖ ❖

Cream separator exhibit at the Union County Fair in Clayton, New Mexico,
September 1914. *(MNM 14623)*

❖ ❖ ❖

Isaacs Hardware Store in Clayton, ca. 1915. *(MNM 14628)*

My Dear Mrs. Campbell:

Mrs. Dillon and I returned to Santa Fe only a day or two ago and the memory of the very pleasant entertainment you gave us at the Amador is still fresh in our minds. It was surely [a] unique experience and a great honor to have the privilege of sleeping in the bed used by Don Benito Juarez, the first president of Mexico.[115]

— *Governor Richard C. Dillon to Mrs. Carina A. Campbell, September 9, 1928*

I think New Mexico was the greatest experience from the outside world that I have ever had. It certainly changed me forever. . . . In the magnificent fierce morning of New Mexico one sprang awake, a new part of the soul woke up suddenly, and the old world gave way to a new.[116]

— *D. H. Lawrence, 1928 or 1929*

On account of the few white visitors in those times the Snake dance was influenced but little by contact with civilization. A religious ceremony it was in the beginning and as such it remained for many years. The automobile has done more to rapidly change the old time West than any other factor; for in little more than ten years it has invaded the most remote corner, and frontier institutions have practically disappeared. . . . The automobile traveller can never know the thrills of riding on horseback mile after mile, hour after hour, across the burning sands under the blazing desert sun; nor can he know the feeling produced by the Snake dance when it was purely a religious ceremony, and he was of ten or fifteen persons present.[117]

— *Author Earle R. Forrest, 1929*

Prayer entered into every action or undertaking. Even in cooking, when starting to mix bread or any food, if you wanted it to come out specially good, the name of the Holy Trinity was invoked. A cross was marked on the bread dough before setting away to rise.[118]

— *Author Cleofas M. Jaramillo, 1941*

❖ ❖ ❖

Adobe *horno* and wooden paddle for removing bread, 1915.
Photo by Kenneth Chapman. *(MNM 28165)*

❖ ❖ ❖

M. C. Pacheco's law office in Taos, New Mexico, ca. 1915. *(MNM 11495)*

❖ ❖ ❖

Steam shovels in Hearst Pit, Santa Rita Copper Mine, August 13, 1916.
Photo probably by Frederick Feldman. *(MNM 65730)*
Enrique L. Romero in Vadito, New Mexico, ca. 1916. *Orlando Romero Collection.*

❖ ❖ ❖

"Mi macho moro y un coyote que cogi" — "My brave white horse and a coyote that I caught."
Cañon de Carrizo near Roy, New Mexico, October 3, 1917.
Mariano Chávez Collection. *(MNM 152908)*
Nina Otero Warren, niece of Solomon Luna, ca. 1920. She was influential in the
Congressional Union, a suffragette organization that campaigned for women's rights
between 1914 and 1920. *(MNM 89756)*

193

❖ ❖ ❖

Ortiz Street, Santa Fe, ca. 1920. Photo by T. Harmon Parkhurst. *(MNM 144777)*

❖ ❖ ❖

Senator Thomas B. Catron, Santa Fe, ca. 1917–1920. Photo by Wesley Bradfield.
(MNM 13309)
Mr. and Mrs. George Heye and Harmon Hendricks visit Santa Fe in 1917, on Palace Avenue
at the corner of the new art museum under construction. George Heye established the Heye
Foundation / Museum of the American Indian in New York.
Photo by Jesse L. Nusbaum. *(MNM 61815)*

❖ ❖ ❖

The Fine Arts Museum in Santa Fe, December 22, 1918.
Photo by Wesley Bradfield. *(MNM 12986)*

During my early childhood, an epidemic of diphtheria swept through the village and took little brother Tomasito. He was dressed in a long lace-trimmed dress and laid on the black round table that stood in the corner of the living room. A wreath of white artificial flowers crowning his fair forehead and a smaller one held his little clasped hands together. José Manuel, the carpenter, made the small board casket; my aunts covered it with pink muslin, trimming it with white lace inside and outside. The family and relatives gathered in the *sala* [kitchen] early in the evening to sing the rosary and hymns. Even the "Our Father," "Hail Mary," and "Glory Patri" were transposed into hymns and sung, for no sad *alabados* were sung at *angelitos'* [little angels'] wakes.[119]

— *Cleofas M. Jaramillo, 1941*

Early in May, Erineo was sent to the sheep camp to help with the lambing. With two leather bags filled with lunch, tied behind the saddle of the black mule, his roll of brown wool (*serape*) tied over it, the cantina filled with fresh spring water and hung from the head of the saddle, he was off. After the shearing, he returned, bringing Mother a roll of long-haired, fine silky goat skins. After the pelts were washed and dried, cooked sheep brains were spread on the wrong side. Then they were set out in the sun until the brains melted and soaked into the skins. The skins were rubbed until soft, then rubbed again with a damp soap. The soap suds were then wiped off, and the goat skin was as white and soft as a chamois.[120]

— *Cleofas M. Jaramillo, 1941*

THE COUNTY OF UNION

Down from the North at an early day,
Bringing the Cash they were willing to pay,
Came Hill and Fox and a dozen more,
And the legislature they went before,
Making a Most ungodly roar
Favoring the County of Union.

In Oath unqualified they swore
They'd spend ten thousand and then ten more,
That the Council should be controlled;
And when the vote was finally polled
Twas found that ten and two was rolled
Up for the County of Union.

Then to the House They all flocked down,
These boomers from young Clayton town:
"We'll have our county or have a fight,
We'll have it whether wrong or right,
For we have money and money is might.
All your pockets with cash we'll fill
If you will only pass the bill
and make the County of Union."

The vote in the House was half and half,
And Union opposers inclined to laugh,
When McMullen of Vegas, in thunder tones,
(How John Hill's face with pleasure shown)
Did change his vote, and that alone,
Carried the County of Union.

Now that Union County is 'stablished at last,
And all the trouble and dissension passed,
We extend to her, as anyone should,
The good right hand of brotherhood;
And may she grow both great and good,
So that her friends may never say
That they have cause to regret the day
They all went down to Santa Fe,
And won the County of Union.[121]

— *Graff W. Abbott, 1936*

❖ ❖ ❖

New Mexico residents, ca. 1920. *(MNM 31841)*

❖ ❖ ❖

Hastiin Klah, Navajo medicine man. Photo by T. Harmon Parkhurst. *(MNM 4330)*

❖ ❖ ❖

José Abel Romero, four years old. Vadito, ca. 1925. *Orlando Romero Collection.*
Raton Pass, ca. 1922. Photo by Ernst Ruth, Sr. *(MNM 85821)*

❖ ❖ ❖

Nathan Jaffa, mayor of Santa Fe (and one-time Acting Governor of New Mexico),
in the courtyard of the Palace of the Governors during Santa Fe Fiesta,
August 2–8, 1925. *(MNM 11779)*

❖ ❖ ❖

Dolly and John Sloan near Santa Fe, 1926. Photo by T. Harmon Parkhurst. *(MNM 28835)*

❖ ❖ ❖

La Bajada Highway Pass between Santa Fe and Albuquerque, ca. 1928.
(SFRC/MNM 92219)

❖ ❖ ❖

"Bog Jack Overalls," Navajo rug, ca. 1930.
Photo by T. Harmon Parkhurst. *(MNM 2723)*

❖ ❖ ❖

Man from Taos Pueblo, ca. 1930. Photo by T. Harmon Parkhurst. *(MNM 22696)*

❖ ❖ ❖

Townsite office in Hobbs, New Mexico, ca. 1930. *(MNM 9366)*
Bronson Cutting, U.S. senator and newspaper publisher, Santa Fe, ca. 1932.
Photo by T. Harmon Parkhurst. *(MNM 51501)*

❖ ❖ ❖

Lobby at the Don Fernando Hotel in Taos, New Mexico, ca. 1930–1935.
Photo by T. Harmon Parkhurst. *(MNM 51596)*

❖ ❖ ❖

Carreta under construction, June 1930. *(MNM 14962)*

❖ ❖ ❖

San Ildefonso Pueblo Eagle Dancers at Seton Village near Santa Fe, 1931.
Photo by Harold Kellogg. *(MNM 77474)*

❖ ❖ ❖

Deer Dancer, San Juan Pueblo, ca. 1930–1935. Photo by
T. Harmon Parkhurst. *(MNM 3860)*

❖ ❖ ❖

Cross of the Martyrs, Santa Fe, ca. 1935. Photo by T. Harmon Parkhurst.
(MNM 51390)

Soon it will be Christmas Eve and Tilano will light the little pitch-wood fire out near the well house to welcome those spirits that draw near on that night. Inside, candles will burn and juniper fragrance will fill the house. Then I shall think of you all and wish that I might share with you the beauty and the peace. The essence of this land fills me at such times — as whenever I give it opportunity — and I know that I have been given more than one human's share of joy.[122]

— *Edith Warner, 1943*

New Year's day of this historic 1945 held no hint of the atomic era. There were no blasts from the Pajarito Plateau making discord in the song of the chorus as I sat in the sun on an old portal at San Ildefonso. Teen, just past two, watched the dancers with me and later demonstrated the steps of the little deer. The only indication of war was the absence of his father and the other young men.[123]

— *Edith Warner, 1945*

"I am become death, the destroyer of worlds."[124]

— *Quoted from* Bhagauad Gita *by J. Robert Oppenheimer at the explosion of the first atom bomb in Alamogordo, New Mexico, July 16, 1945*

I was born to desperately poor people, but I am not shamed to relate this because my father and mother took care of me to their best means and efforts. They make their living by farming, which in speaking was very small the crops they raised. Most all the crops were consumed for family use. I did not realize it until I was six years old when I was able to reason, after my senses were alerted, I realized my parents were very poor. At times we were unable to obtain food from stores and ate food made of corn. I was not furnished with expensive clothes. During summer I went barefooted with a thin manta shirt which my mother made.[125]

— *Roland Duran, Picurís Pueblo, 1956*

Murals painted by Randall Davey for his wife's dressing room, Santa Fe, ca. 1935.
Photo by T. Harmon Parkhurst. *(MNM 32104)*

❖ ❖ ❖

Richard Martínez, artist of San Ildefonso Pueblo, ca. 1935.
Photo by T. Harmon Parkhurst. *(MNM 4029)*

❖ ❖ ❖

Penitente death figure, Las Trampas, ca. 1935. Photo by T. Harmon Parkhurst.
(MNM 11529)

❖ ❖ ❖

Córdova, New Mexico, ca. 1930. Photo by T. Harmon Parkhurst. *(MNM 2757)*

❖ ❖ ❖

Navajo mother and child. Photo by T. Harmon Parkhurst. *(MNM 55191)*

❖ ❖ ❖

Governor Clyde Tingley with his car at the Governor's Mansion, Santa Fe, 1936.
(MNM 50497)

❖ ❖ ❖

Winter in Truchas, New Mexico, February 20, 1939. *(MNM 11580)*
Main Conchas Dam (view from the southwest), ca. 1938–1939. Photo by U.S. Corps
of Engineers. *(MNM 59160)*

❖ ❖ ❖

Embudo Canyon on the Rio Grande, ca. 1940. Photo by T. Harmon Parkhurst.
(MNM 67896)

❖ ❖ ❖

Child of Eleutario Suina in dance costume at Cochiti Pueblo.
Photo by T. Harmon Parkhurst. *(MNM 69985)*

❖ ❖ ❖

George López, woodcarver, Córdova, New Mexico, ca. 1940.
Photo by T. Harmon Parkhurst. *(MNM 9973)*

❖ ❖ ❖

Scene in the Valle Grande, in the Jémez Mountains. Photo by T. Harmon Parkhurst.
(MNM 68914)

❖ ❖ ❖

Flock of sheep. Photo by T. Harmon Parkhurst. *(MNM 51462)*

❖ ❖ ❖

Kossa clowns, San Juan Pueblo, ca. 1940. Photo by T. Harmon Parkhurst.
(MNM 3895)

❖ ❖ ❖

The burning of Zozobra, Santa Fe Fiesta, ca. 1950. *(MNM 47327)*

❖ ❖ ❖

Cloud formation, White Sands, New Mexico, ca. 1948. Infrared photo by Leon Cantrell.
(MNM 56482)
The first atomic bomb at Trinity Site, White Sands, New Mexico, July 16, 1945.
Photo by Los Alamos National Laboratory (#653994). *(MNM 71128)*

We were greatly helped by my grandmother Manuelita who was [a] *medica* and assisted and gave medicine to the sick. She was known in that locality for her good medicine. She did not charge on her medicine, but earned flour, meat, food stuff. Many times I accompanied her in such places as Chamisal, Llano, Largo, Vadito, Penasco. Sometimes we stayed three or four days. In those days there were no doctors, only *medicas* who practiced medicine made of herbs, leaves and roots.[126]

— *Roland Duran, Picurís Pueblo, 1956*

During the time I lived in the old Lincoln County courthouse, in my capacity as State Historian of New Mexico, the interest shown in the bloody career of this little outlaw was a matter of continuing wonder to me. The first question asked by most tourists, young and old, and whatever degree of intelligence was usually, "Show me the balcony from which Billy the Kid leaped, manacled hand and foot, onto a bucking horse to make his escape."[127]

— *Governor George Curry, 1958*

In New Mexico whatever is both old and peculiar appears upon examination to have a connection with arid climate. Peculiarities range from the striking adaptation of the flora onwards to those of the fauna, and on up to those of the human animal.[128]

— *Author Ross Calvin, 1965*

[T]he unbiased reader can hardly fail to agree that sky determined the general character of plant life and animal life in the arid Southwest, and influenced the history of its various populations and shaped their cultures until the resources of twentieth-century science afforded partial control of the waters.[129]

— *Ross Calvin, 1965*

❖ ❖ ❖

María Martínez preparing to fire pottery at San Ildefonso, ca. 1950.
Photo by Tyler Dingee. *(MNM 73449)*

❖ ❖ ❖

Nuestra Señora del Rosario, la Conquistadora. Photo by Tyler Dingee, 1951.
(MNM 73832)

❖ ❖ ❖

Monument at the site of Oñate's first capital, established in 1598 and named San Juan
de los Cabelleros. Photo ca. 1950. *(MNM 16739)*
A Cockroft-Walton Injector at the Los Alamos Meson Physics Facility.
Photo by Los Alamos Laboratory (#707734). *(MNM 52341)*

❖ ❖ ❖

Woman trapper, ca. 1950. Rives Studio Collection. *(RGHC A74-61)*

❖ ❖ ❖

Manuel Apodaca, Santa Fe blacksmith, 1958.
Photo by Bob La Rouche. *(MNM 6996)*

Today the progeny of the Conquistadores is a mixed race, backward, illiterate, poor — disinherited in the land of their fathers. They retain a mellow quaintness — because they cannot help it.[130]

— *Ross Calvin, 1965*

So the pageant has for its setting the intoxicating splendor of the desert, the green magnificence of the forest, the mystery of barbaric mountains, the serene openness of a sky whose eye is the desert-making sun.[131]

— *Ross Calvin, 1965*

After all we Hispanic New Mexicans are all Penitentes in some way, through blood origins and landscape and a long history of suffering.[132]

— *Fray Angélico Chávez, 1974*

Here in this little place in the countryside of New Mexico and its environs lived many families, and one could see that the people were very joyful and happy. I believe this to be because every living thing worked to make a living, many in the open air which is so good for health.[133]

— *On the village of Guadalupita, Louisa Torres, 1978*

When I was thirteen I saw a man drunk for the first time. He said to my father, "Wheat is the best thing and the worst thing. And I will prove it to you: wheat makes the Host which is changed into the body and blood of Jesus Christ and also the liquor which makes us so drunk."[134]

— *Louisa Torres, 1978*

The other item in the pouch was a simple message on buckskin inviting all Pueblo officials and their people to assemble for a historic meeting at Santa Domingo Pueblo, with Spanish, Mexican and state officials, for the purpose of exchanging gifts, renewing historical ties, and for the reinforcement of Pueblo sovereignty recognized by the Spaniards in the seventeenth century.[135]

— *On the Tricentennial Celebration of the Pueblo Indian Revolt, Herman Agoyo, 1980*

❖ ❖ ❖

Musicians and Matachina Dancers at Chimayó, New Mexico, 1964.
Photo by Marian F. Love. *(MNM 102409)*

❖ ❖ ❖

Doris, granddaughter of Juan Poncho, costumed for the Corn Dance at Cochiti Pueblo,
July 14, 1969. Photo by Bart Durham. *(MNM 45474)*

This feeling of brotherhood, of oneness so strong 300 years ago, emerged once again as the runners entered each village where other runners waited nervously to be part of the link; the spirit was interpreted at the end by a group of Hopi elders during a smoking ceremony when they said the run was like "opening a door" uniting us as Pueblo people. The door was now open to continually "think of each other, to gain long life, more rain, and an abundance of crops."[136]

— *On the Tricentennial Celebration of the Pueblo Indian Revolt, Herman Agoyo, 1980*

The frontier experience has long been considered a major contributor to the development of American ideals and attitudes. New Mexico is unique among states in having a frontier heritage that lasted over 300 years. In fact, no place in North America experienced the process longer. Most areas were frontiers for only the first years of their existence and then the frontier moved further west or north.[137]

— *Introduction label for "The Frontier Experience: New Mexico 1598–1900,"*
an exhibit in the Palace of the Governors, 1978

His name is Robert Duck. And, for the second year in a row, he has carried away the $1,500 first-place prize from the Great American Duck Race.

Duck, who is from Bosque Farms near Albuquerque, doesn't do much running himself. But he raises and trains the fastest ducks in New Mexico. . . .

Asked his secret, Duck said, "I tickle them a little and get them excited and then just let them go."

The Great American Duck Race was begun in 1980 after a group of businessmen decided this southern New Mexico town of 12,000 needed more excitement. The event has turned into Deming's biggest tourist attraction, drawing thousands of people each year.

Since its beginnings as a simple race between feathered finishers, more events have been added. This year human contestants participated in a "Tortilla Toss," won by James Cannizzo of Deming, who flung the flat corn disk 322 feet.

Presiding over it all was this year's Duck Queen, Ann Novak of Deming, who was bedecked in yellow feathers and orange beak and feet.

Chief Quacker Bernie Green said this is the last year the event will be handled by the tiny committee that has staged it since the beginning.

"The chamber of commerce is taking it over," Green said. "We're ducking out. We've gone quackers."[138]

— The Santa Fe New Mexican, *August 23, 1982*

Las Cruces — A world's record was claimed at the 2nd annual Whole Enchilada Festival Sunday as a six and a half foot enchilada was cooked and served to a cheering crowd on the city's Downtown Mall.

The enchilada, a three-layer concoction of corn tortillas, onions, cheese and very hot red Mesilla Valley chili sauce, exceeded by a foot and a half last year's five-foot record setter.

And this time, Robert Estrada and Jack Corder hope it will be accepted as a legitimate mark and included in the next edition of the *Guinness Book of World Records.*

"We tried to get last year's enchilada into the book," Corder said, as the 45-pound tortillas were cooking, "but the publishers said Spanish food was not popular enough around the world to be included in their book."[139]

— The Albuquerque Journal, *October 4, 1982*

Those murals at Peña Blanca have no artistic merit whatsoever.[140]

— *Father Jerome Martínez, assistant to Archbishop Robert Sánchez,*
September 1986 (one month before the demolition of the murals
and the church at Peña Blanca)

If no one knows (a building) exists then why not let it go back to the earth from which it came? Why not respect the church for what it was and leave it at that?[141]

— *Father Jerome Martínez,* The Santa Fe New Mexican, *January 25, 1987*

❖ ❖ ❖

"Winter Pasture," Cienega, New Mexico, 1982. Photo by Art Taylor.
(Courtesy the photographer)

❖ ❖ ❖

Santa Fe Chamber Music Festival artists on their way to rehearsal. Photograph from a flier
for the Santa Fe Chamber Music Festival. *(Courtesy the Santa Fe Chamber Music Festival)*
Shuttle landing at White Sands, New Mexico. Photo by NASA.

241

❖ ❖ ❖

"Jesus Meets Veronica." Detail of the Stations of the Cross, done as frescoes (now demolished)
at Peña Blanca by Fray Angélico Chávez. Painted in 1942. Local people were used as models for
characters of the Passion. Depicted are Anastacio Quintana, Clotilde Ortiz, Rebecca Ortiz,
Leonor Ortiz, and Tranquilino De La O. Photo by Charles Bennett (privately owned).

Notes

1. George P. Hammond and Agapito Rey, eds., *Narratives of the Coronado Expedition, 1540–1542* (Albuquerque: University of New Mexico Press, 1942), pp. 180–181.

2. Hammond and Rey, *Narratives,* p. 203.

3. Hammond and Rey, *Narratives,* p. 202.

4. Hammond and Rey, *Narratives,* p. 181.

5. Hammond and Rey, *Narratives,* pp. 256–257.

6. Hammond and Rey, *Narratives,* pp. 261–262.

7. George P. Hammond and Agapito Rey, eds., *The Rediscovery of New Mexico, 1580–1594* (Albuquerque: University of New Mexico Press, 1966), pp. 67–68.

8. Hammond and Rey, *Rediscovery,* p. 78.

9. Hammond and Rey, *Rediscovery,* p. 78.

10. Hammond and Rey, *Rediscovery,* p. 299.

11. Hammond and Rey, *Rediscovery,* p. 316.

12. Hammond and Rey, *Rediscovery,* p. 317.

13. George P. Hammond and Agapito Rey, eds., *Don Juan de Oñate: Colonizer of New Mexico, 1595–1628,* vol. I (Albuquerque: University of New Mexico Press, 1953), pp. 62–63.

14. Hammond and Rey, *Oñate,* p. 67.

15. Hammond and Rey, *Oñate,* p. 613.

16. Hammond and Rey, *Oñate,* vol. II, p. 1065.

17. Irene L. Chávez, trans., "Velasco's Orders to Don Pedro de Peralta," *New Mexico Historical Review,* vol. IV, no. 2 (April 1929), pp. 185–186.

18. Gaspar Pérez de Villagrá, *History of New Mexico,* trans. Gilberto Espinoza, (Los Angeles: The Quivira Society, 1933), p. 156.

19. Lansing B. Bloom, "A Glimpse of New Mexico in 1620," *New Mexico Historical Review,* vol. III, no. 4 (July 1928) pp. 366–367.

20. Fray Zárate Salmerón, *Relaciones,* ed. and trans. Alicia Ronstadt Milich (Albuquerque: Horn & Wallace Publishers, 1966), pp. 100–101.

21. Fray Alonso de Benavides, *Benavides' Memorial of 1630,* trans. Peter P. Forrestal, C.S.C. (Washington, D.C.: Academy of American Franciscan History, 1954), p. 8.

22. Benavides, *Memorial,* p. 38.

23. Benavides, *Memorial,* p. 41.

24. Benavides, *Memorial,* p. 58.

25. Benavides, *Memorial,* p. 59.

26. Benavides, *Memorial,* p. 35.

27. Benavides, *Memorial,* p. 36.

28. France Scholes, "Troublous Times in New Mexico, 1659–1670," *New Mexico Historical Review,* vol. XII, no. 4 (October 1937), p. 436.

29. Scholes, "Troublous Times," vol. XVI, no. 1 (January 1941), p. 26.

30. As quoted in Fray Angélico Chávez, "Nuestra Señora de la Macana," *New Mexico Historical Review,* vol. XXXIV, no. 2 (April 1959), p. 85.

31. Charmon Clair Shelby, ed. and trans., *Revolt of the Pueblo Indians of New Mexico and Otermin's Reconquest, 1680–1682* (Albuquerque: University of New Mexico Press, 1970), p. 3.

32. J. Manuel Espinosa, *First Expedition of Vargas into New Mexico, 1692* (Albuquerque: University of New Mexico Press, 1940), p. 103.

33. Espinosa, *First Expedition,* p. 105.

34. Archivo General de Indias, Guadalajara, Legajo 139.

35. Alfred Barnaby Thomas, *After Coronado: Spanish Exploration Northeast of New Mexico, 1696–1727* (Norman: University of Oklahoma Press, 1935), pp. 184–185.

36. Alfred Barnaby Thomas, *The Plains Indians and New Mexico, 1751–1778* (Albuquerque: University of New Mexico Press, 1940), pp. 76–77.

37. Thomas, *Plains Indians,* pp. 117–118.

38. Thomas, *Plains Indians,* p. 108.

39. Eleanor B. Adams, ed., *Bishop Tamarón's Visitation of New Mexico, 1760* (Albuquerque: University of New Mexico Press and Historical Society of New Mexico, 1954), p. 28.

40. Adams, *Tamarón,* pp. 50–51.

41. Adams, *Tamarón,* p. 30.

42. Don Pedro Alonso O'Crowley, *A Description of the Kingdom of New Spain,* ed. and trans. Seán Galvin (San Francisco: John Howell, 1972), p. 55.

43. Fray Angélico Chávez and Eleanor B. Adams, *The Missions of New Mexico* (Albuquerque: University of New Mexico Press, 1956), p. 151.

44. Chávez and Adams, *Missions,* p. 252.

45. Chávez and Adams, *Missions,* p. 151.

46. Chávez and Adams, *Missions,* p. 4.

47. Chávez and Adams, *Missions,* p. 4.

48. Alfred Barnaby Thomas, ed., *Forgotton Frontiers: A Study of the Spanish Indian Policy of Don Juan Bautista De Anza, Governor of New Mexico, 1777–1787* (Norman: University of Oklahoma Press, 1932), p. 145.

49. Noel P. Loomis and Abraham P. Nasatir, *Pedro Vial and the Roads to Santa Fe* (Norman: University of Oklahoma Press, 1967), p. 413.

50. Loomis and Nasatir, *Vial,* p. 411.

51. Loomis and Nasatir, *Vial,* p. 417.

52. Loomis and Nasatir, *Vial,* p. 424.

53. Milo Milton Quaife, ed., *The Southwestern Expedition of Zebulon M. Pike* (Chicago: The Lakeside Press, 1925), p. 136.

54. Quaife, *Pike,* pp. 149–150.

55. Quaife, *Pike,* p. 152.

56. H. Bailey Carroll and J. Villasana Haggard, *Three New Mexico Chronicles* (Albuquerque: The Quivira Society, 1942), p. 36.

57. Carroll and Haggard, *Chronicles,* p. 59.

58. Carroll and Haggard, *Chronicles,* p. 67.

59. Mexican Archives of New Mexico, State Records Center and Archives, Santa Fe.

60. Mexican Archives of New Mexico.

61. Carroll and Haggard, *Chronicles,* p. 95.

62. Carroll and Haggard, *Chronicles,* p. 54.

63. Manuel Alvarez Papers, Ledger Book 1834, State Records Center and Archives, Santa Fe.

64. W.H.H. Allison, "Santa Fe as It Appeared During the Winter of the Years 1837 and 1838," *Old Santa Fe,* vol. II (October 1914), pp. 176–177.

65. Allison, "Santa Fe," p. 178.

66. "Tourist in Santa Fe, 1840: Sketches by Matthew C. Field, From the Files of the New Orleans Picayune," *El Palacio,* vol. 66, no. 1 (February 1959), p. 29.

67. Josiah Gregg, *Commerce of the Prairies,* ed. Max. L. Moorhead (Norman: University of Oklahoma Press, 1954), p. 78.

68. Gregg, *Commerce of the Prairies,* p. 155.

69. Gregg, *Commerce of the Prairies,* p. 171.

70. Gregg, *Commerce of the Prairies,* p. 142.

71. Stella M. Drumm, ed., *Down the Santa Fe Trail and Into Mexico: The Diary of Susan Shelby Magoffin, 1846–1847* (New Haven: Yale University Press, 1926), pp. 130–131.

72. Drumm, *Diary,* pp. 137–138.

73. Drumm, *Diary,* p. 165.

74. Drumm, *Diary,* pp. 173–174.

75. Lewis H. Garrard, *Wah-to-yah and the Taos Trail* (Norman: University of Oklahoma Press, 1955), p. 173.

76. George Archibald McCall, *New Mexico in 1850: A Military View,* ed. Robert Frazer (Norman: University of Oklahoma Press, 1968), pp. 82–83.

77. McCall, *New Mexico in 1850,* p. 86.

78. Anne Heloise Abel, ed., "The Journal of John Greiner," *Old Santa Fe,* vol. III, no. 11 (July 1916), p. 197.

79. Abel, "Journal," p. 202.

80. Abel, "Journal," p. 203.

81. Abel, "Journal," p. 210.

82. Edward D. Tittman, "By Order of Richard Campbell," *New Mexico Historical Review,* vol. III, no. 4 (October 1928), p. 392.

83. Blanche C. Grant, ed., *Kit Carson's Own Story of His Life* (Taos: Kit Carson Memorial Foundation, 1926), pp. 117–118.

84. Grant, *Carson's Own Story,* p. 122.

85. Transcribed in the Las Cruces vertical file, History Library, Palace of the Governors.

86. Las Cruces file, History Library, Palace of the Governors.

87. John P. Clum, "Es-kim-In-Zin," *New Mexico Historical Review,* vol. III, no. 4 (October 1928), p. 401.

88. *The Santa Fe Daily New Mexican,* June 24, 1873.

89. As quoted in John P. Wilson, *Merchants, Guns and Money: The Story of Lincoln County and Its Wars* (Santa Fe: Museum of New Mexico Press, 1987), p. 63.

90. Lloyd Lewis, *Sherman: Fighting Prophet* (New York: Harcourt and Brace, 1936), p. 596.

91. *The Santa Fe New Mexican,* February 27, 1880.

92. *The Santa Fe New Mexican,* October 28, 1880.

93. Averam B. Bender, *The March of Empire* (Lawrence: University of Kansas Press, 1952), p. 154.

94. James T. Stensvaag, "Clio on the Frontier: The Intellectual Evolution of the History Society of New Mexico, 1858–1925," *New Mexico Historical Review,* vol. 55, no. 4 (1980), p. 299.

95. *The Santa Fe New Mexican,* October 8, 1881.

96. Adolf F. Bandelier, *The Southwestern Journals of Adolph F. Bandelier, 1880–1882,* ed. Charles H. Lange and Carroll L. Riley (Albuquerque: University of New Mexico Press, 1966), p. 183.

97. Morris B. Parker, *White Oaks: Life in a New Mexico Gold Camp, 1880–1900,* ed. C. L. Sonnichsen (Tucson: University of Arizona Press, 1971), p. 30.

98. Parker, *White Oaks,* pp. 38–39.

99. William G. Ritch, comp., *The New Mexico Bluebook, 1882,* facsimile edition (Albuquerque: University of New Mexico Press, 1968), p. 49.

100. Ritch, *Bluebook,* p. 12A.

101. Ritch, *Bluebook,* p. 12.

102. Miguel Antonio Otero, *My Life on the Frontier, 1882–1897,* vol. II (Albuquerque: University of New Mexico Press, 1939), p. 33.

103. Robert W. Larson, *New Mexico's Quest for Statehood, 1846–1912* (Albuquerque: University of New Mexico Press, 1968), p. 141.

104. Charles Lummis, *The Land of Poco Tiempo* (Albuquerque: University of New Mexico Press, 1952), p. 6.

105. Lummis, *The Land of Poco Tiempo,* pp. 38–39.

106. Lummis, *The Land of Poco Tiempo,* pp. 12–13.

107. Lummis, *The Land of Poco Tiempo,* p. 61.

108. Lummis, *The Land of Poco Tiempo,* p. 224.

109. *The New Mexico Sentinel,* January 26, 1938, Las Cruces vertical file, History Library, Palace of the Governors.

110. *The Santa Fe New Mexican,* November 21, 1910.

111. *The Santa Fe New Mexican,* June 20, 1912.

112. Harold Palmer Brown, "Assignment: Villa Raid," *El Palacio,* vol. 86, no. 3 (Fall 1980), p. 5.

113. *The Santa Fe New Mexican,* September 7, 1918.

114. *The Albuquerque Journal,* June 16, 1926.

115. Las Cruces vertical file, History Library, Palace of the Governors.

116. Edward D. McDonald, ed., *Phoenix: The Posthumous Papers of D. H. Lawrence* (New York: Viking Press, 1936), p. 142.

117. Earle R. Forrest, *Missions and Pueblos of the Old Southwest* (Glorieta: The Rio Grande Press, 1979), p. 279.

118. Cleofas M. Jaramillo, *Shadows of the Past* (Santa Fe: Seton Village Press, 1941), p. 26.

119. Jaramillo, *Shadows of the Past,* p. 35.

120. Jaramillo, *Shadows of the Past,* p. 42.

121. Union County file, May 13, 1936, History Library, Palace of the Governors.

122. Peggy Pond Church, *The House at Otowi Bridge: The Story of Edith Warner and Los Alamos* (Albuquerque: University of New Mexico Press, 1966), p. 125.

123. Church, *Otowi Bridge,* p. 128.

124. John Bartlett, *Familiar Quotations,* 15th edition (Boston: Little Brown and Co., 1980), p. 861.

125. Donald N. Brown, "Roland Duran, Man of Picuris," *El Palacio,* vol. 87, no. 4 (Winter 1981–82), pp. 3–4.

126. Brown, "Duran," p. 4.

127. Governor George Curry, *George Curry, 1861–1947: An Autobiography* (Albuquerque: University of New Mexico Press, 1958), p. 44.

128. Ross Calvin, *Sky Determines: An Interpretation of the Southwest* (Albuquerque: University of New Mexico Press, 1965), p. ix.

129. Calvin, *Sky Determines,* p. xiii.

130. Calvin, *Sky Determines,* p. 7.

131. Calvin, *Sky Determines,* p. 7.

132. Fray Angélico Chávez, *My Penitente Land: Reflections of Spanish New Mexico* (Albuquerque: University of New Mexico Press, 1974), p. xiv.

133. Gioia Brandi, comp., "The Words of an Old One," *El Palacio,* vol. 84, no. 3 (Fall 1978), p. 9.

134. Brandi, "Old One," p. 10.

135. Introduction label, "The Frontier Experience: New Mexico 1598–1900," exhibit in the Palace of the Governors, 1978.

136. Herman Agoyo, "The Tricentennial Year in Pueblo Consciousness," *El Palacio,* vol. 86, no. 4 (Winter 1980–81), p. 29.

137. Agoyo, "Tricentennial," p. 30.

138. *The Santa Fe New Mexican,* August 23, 1982.

139. *The Albuquerque Journal,* October 4, 1982.

140. Michael Moquin, "The Adobe Quagmire: New Mexico's Endangered Churches," *Traditions Southwest,* vol. 1, no. 1 (Fall 1989), p. 24.

141. *The Santa Fe New Mexican,* January 25, 1987.

Index